RENÉ LA SAGNE

Ex-Foreign Legion Catering Corps chef René La Sagne – now a celebrity restaurateur, and The Prince of Mince – teaches ex-Legionnaire Serge, the art of the kitchen.

René says: "It is strange that with such brave men, many find a kitchen to be a No Man's Land. I can help men conquer their fears – by telling them something of my world. A kitchen can be a command post and a power base – and if basic training can be mastered, and survival skills are learned, there is no need to starve in the field, or be forced to exist on pre-packed rations."

From buttered toast to dinner party host – Serge goes over the top, survives and learns how to command his own culinary respect.

René La Sagne's

THE KITCHEN ASSAULT COURSE FOR MEN

… WHO CAN'T COOK — OR HAVE NEVER HAD TO!

WAVERLEY BOOKS

The Kitchen Assault Course For Men by René La Sagne

First published 2010, by Waverley Books Ltd,
144 Port Dundas Road, Glasgow,
G4 0HZ, Scotland

Selected recipes are from *The Glasgow Cookery Book*,
© Glasgow Caledonian University, published by Waverley Books.

Photographs by arrangement with Shutterstock.
Page 17 Legion picture.
by arrangement with the Press Association/PA Photos Limited

Design and illustration by Hugo Breingan

ISBN 978 1 84934 000 7

Printed and bound in the EU
Typeset in Bitstream Futura BT

A catalogue for this book is
available from the British Library

1 2 3 4 5 6 7 8 9 10

"LE BOUDIN"

Boudin is a kind of blood sausage, made of pork, pig's blood and other ingredients. Boudin is also the name given to the Legionnaires' blanket rolls. "Le Boudin" is the French Foreign Legion's marching song. Here is the beginning:

> Tiens, voilà du boudin, voilà du boudin, voilà du
> boudin
> Pour les Alsaciens, les Suisses et les Lorrains;
> Pour les Belges y'en a plus, [twice]
> Ce sont des tireurs au cul.
> Pour les Belges y'en a plus, [twice]
> Ce sont des tireurs au cul.
>
> Nous sommes des dégourdis, nous sommes des
> lascars,
> Des types pas ordinaires,
> Nous avons souvent notre cafard,
> Nous sommes des Légionnaires.

> *Here you are, some blood pudding, some blood*
> *pudding, some blood pudding*
> *For the Alsatians, the Swiss and the Lorrains;*
> *For the Belgians there's none left, [twice]*
> *They're lazy so and so's.*
> *For the Belgians there's none left, [twice]*
> *They're lazy so and so's.*
>
> *We're at ease, we're rough-and-tough,*
> *No ordinary guys,*
> *We've often got our black moods,*
> *We are Legionnaires.*

CONTENTS

Serge's storecupboard

"WIND OF MY SOUPS AND
MEATBALLS TRAVELLED FAR"

I am not a military man. When I was called up for National Service after I moved to France, they wanted A1 candidates. I was graded 2F2F – Too Fat To Fight.

This, for me, was a blessing. I am Swiss, by birth. Neutral.

I served in the Catering Corps before I went to the great kitchens in Paris to really learn my trade. I still meet some of my comrades, who tell stories of their great struggles on the front lines of battle – brave men all, many have been decorated. But what they all have in common is that they all have to eat.

My role in the Corps was to help feed battalions. I know what it is like to feed the Five Thousand. Wind of my soups and meatballs travelled far. I was poached by the French Foreign Legion.

Serge, my head waiter, was a Legionnaire. Serge is short for Sergeant. But he is not short.

The Foreign Legion is known as a crack military unit whose training focuses on the military skills you would expect, but also it is very strong on what we call esprit de corps. The Legion has come through several Republics, an empire, two World Wars, the rise and fall of conscription, the dismantling of a colonial empire and, of course, the French loss of the Legion's birthplace – Algeria. Its soldiers come from far and wide, from many different countries each with different cultures and tastes, so catering for such an elite without causing mutiny was something of a headache.

But even for such brave men, something I realised is that so many of them find a kitchen to be a No Man's Land, a minefield, territory to be avoided.

It is my role to help men conquer their kitchen fears, by telling them of my world – a world filled with stirring stories, by teaching them through these pages, as I was taught, that a kitchen is a command post – it is a power base. I tell them that if basic training is mastered, and basic survival skills are learned, you will not starve in the field, or be forced to exist on pre-packed rations.

The respect which will be gained can bring rewards greater than any you can imagine.

I now use my Maison de Mince as Operational HQ. I taught Serge the love of cooking here when he tracked me down after leaving the Legion. He couldn't go back to France. He needed to find a job, and just like with the Legion, he needed to start a new life. He wanted to learn the wonders of the pan and the grill.

I had to agree – you don't turn your back or close your door on a fellow Legionnaire.

This book is a Legionnaire's guide for everyman. You too can cook like an ex-Legionnaire. I will show you all about everything including le boudin.

Boudin is a kind of blood sausage. Le boudin to the common Legionnaire meant the blanket roll carried on top of their backpacks. "Le Boudin" is the official march of the French Foreign Legion.

The song makes reference to the fact that the Belgians don't get any "blood sausage", because the King of Belgium at the time refused to allow any Belgian citizens to join the Legion. To this day, we don't serve Belgians with le boudin at the Maison de Mince. It's about respect.

All ranks of the Legion sing "Le Boudin" standing to attention.

When they march, the French Foreign Legion marches at only 88 steps per minute, much slower than the 120 steps per minute of all other French military units. This is why the Legion's representatives at Bastille Day are seen marching at the back of the parade, and why service at Maison de Mince is a little slower than in fast-food restaurants.

And in this book you have from Serge some advice about wine.

The French Foreign Legion has had a vineyard at Puyloubier in Provence, near Aix-en-Provence, for a very long time. Legionnaires who have been retired or invalided out of active service can work there. In Provence they make several hundred thousand bottles of red, rosé and white wine, which keeps the Legion's messes across the world from going dry. The wine is of course called "Esprit de Corps".

The wines have been described as "Strong when attacked, solid on the onslaught, full of grapeshot on the front line".

Serge spent time there. He knows his wines, and still uses his 5-in-1 Foreign Legion Chow Set to open the wine bottles – even those with screwtops. Serge is enthusiastic.

"IN THE KITCHEN YOU PLAY WITH FIRE, AND JUGGLE WITH KNIVES"

I sat with Serge for many evenings after we had turned the "Fermé" sign round on the door of Maison de Mince, pulled down the blind, and pulled a cork or two. I really must make a new sign to stop people knocking on the door after hours. They don't recognise "Fermé" here. So we sit in the dark with the blinds down.

There were some tears (as I peeled onions of course). Legionnaires don't cry so easily.

I listened to his story but I can't repeat it. Only he can tell you. I don't know when he decided he wanted to become a chef like me, but I am honoured that he came.

I explained to Serge that it is impossible to learn the whole subject of my craft from one small book, as in fact you never stop learning, and if it was so easy, why would I have spent so many years in hot kitchens being shouted at and beaten with spoons? But, to be honest, once you know some basic methods, cooking is very much a matter of common sense – but you need to use your imagination too. You don't need to know everything – but you can survive and command respect if you can master a few dishes in the kitchen, and then gradually increase your repertoire to impress.

I bought Serge a *Glasgow Cookery Book,* the book of the Dough School. It is now his Bible. He reads it at his pillow, as I did mine. It is not in Scottish language, it is in English. I had one at the front, sold to me by a Scottish Legionnaire from Partick's Thistle. His name is Mr Shuggie Toyoubytheway. Mr Shuggie Toyoubytheway comes to my restaurant still.

Sometimes he brings other Shuggies by the way.

It was this book of the Dough which helped the Legion. It tells you how to provide for an army. Whether you have a petit army or a grand army.

I tell everyone always to be prepared to try new foods and new combinations of foods. We experts sometimes call this fusion when we take food from different cultures and present them on a plate. Sometimes it is con fusion as we say en France.

Many people like apple sauce with roast pork, but try frying apple rings with a boudin sausage for breakfast. The greatest sausage in the world is

of course le boudin. In this book I take you to this great height. I teach you the secret of the sausage as a pinnacle. It is my Matterhorn.

And – you must realise that I am an artist too. Remember that it is important to make food look appetising. The old saying "the proof of the boudin is in the eating" may be true enough, but if food is nicely served it adds to the enjoyment and people will want to try it. Colour is very important. A meal of steamed fish, boiled potatoes and cauliflower coated with white sauce might be nourishing, but think how dreary it would look. A little parsley and lemon on the fish, perhaps some tomatoes, peas instead of cauliflower, or both, and some chopped parsley on the potatoes makes so much difference.

None of the dishes in this book are really difficult or complicated to make, but do not be in despair if one does not turn out perfectly the first time you try it. There is no need to throw things and break the place up. Think what could have gone wrong, then try again another time.

As a chef des armées, I had special responsibility to feed the front line. It was of paramount importance that those rations which I served would keep our brave Legionnaires strong and healthy. Even if you do not live in a trench this basic knowledge is très important.

So – we have a Swiss in the French Foreign Legion, with a *Glasgow Cookery Book* – what more could an army hope for?

"THERE ARE THINGS ABOUT FOOD AND EATING THAT YOU NEED TO UNDERSTAND"

Don't despair about recipes. They are just instructions. No different from putting a model aircraft together. No different from assembling flat-pack furniture made by the Swedish. No different from a railway timetable – just a logical progression from one station to another.

There are things about Legionnaires that you need to understand. There are things about food and eating that you need to understand.

THINGS THAT HAVE TO BE UNDERSTOOD

NOSE TO TAIL

When I began to teach Serge it was easier to explain things if we imagined a military approach, and I think this is a good way for men to learn something of the culinary world. But there was not always the budget in the war zone to provide everything that I wanted to, and more often than not supplies became disrupted, so we had to be very creative and resourceful. Not unlike the times we live in today. We could not waste anything. So in this book I spend some time in guiding you to eating "nose-to-tail".

I read that one-in-five Britons have taken notice of cheaper cuts of meat, including offal, in the past few years. There has been a large increase in sales, the highest rise in the red meat category for decades.

So I say to you – take heart, these less popular cuts can be really delicious, as well as being nutritious. Imagine a tender oxtail stew melting in your mouth. Subtle sweetbreads – creamy sauce. Merveilleux!

Apparently the word "offal" comes from "off fall" – meaning the bits that fall off or out of the poor beast that has just been slaughtered. I think that's tripe – just a load of bollocks. Never mind. I prefer the term "the fifth quarter" – it so makes me think of my Paris – the 5th Arrondissement – the best-known of the city's districts – the Left Bank of the River Seine. It is also known as the "Latin Quarter" (le quartier Latin), because the first great Parisian university, the Sorbonne, was founded there and Latin was the language the medieval students used to speak, to order their offal – *exta, -orum* meaning 'the entrails'. "Can I have my offal exta orum please?"

En France, we know all about offal, or triperie. It is the term which collectively describes tripe, tongue, trotters, testicles and the various other sheep cow, pig and other animal bits. En France they take the bull by the balls.

Offal from poultry or birds is known as giblets, and I read somewhere that in olden times in England that they used to call triperie "umbles". And this is where the expression "humble pie" comes from – and we say to eat humble pie when we are apologetic and accept something and go back on our point of view. Serge and I have a recipe for Humble Pie (see page 153).

In America they talk about "variety meats" – instead of using the offal word. I don't know why. Serge said to me, "So why don't more people cook offal?"

I looked gravely at him and replied, "It is fear and lack of knowledge. But it is the hard times which have brought it back to fashion. Tripe, tongues, sweetbreads, oxtails, kidneys and hearts. You have to try it. You can make a pig's ear of it very happily. I can show you."

We spoke about nutrition and how offal has much to recommend it, and how it makes a low-budget meal. The taste is also extraordinary – it can be meaty with a mushroom texture, or it can have a strong, gamey flavour, but it is a little tricky to prepare.

Apart from Kelly Marie, Paisley's own disco diva, my favourite singer is Cilla Black – we Legionnaires were moved by her "Anyone Who Had A Heart".

So – don't be afraid – be tempted! Liver. Pig's and lamb's liver. Excellent fried in olive oil and served with gravy. Try tender ox tongue, gently simmered in a light beef stock with root vegetables and herbs.

You can be creative – use your brains.

My Legionnaires know that offal is rich in protein – important for the immune system, energy and healthy cell growth and well-being. Heart, liver and kidneys are a wonderful source of iron. Offal also contains B vitamins, which are required for a healthy blood and nervous system.

Liver is rich in Vitamin A, vital for growth, reproduction, and healthy skin, complexion, hair and eyes.

Liver and kidneys are both high in cholesterol, but just like the cholesterol in eggs and seafood, the body can break it all down quite easily. Offal is not expensive – talk to your local butcher.

So, why not try offal? It's worth exploring.

But, if you don't want an adventure with offal, there is plenty of other food to get your teeth into in my book. My adventure with offal is only small parts. And if people argue with you – simply avoid the discussion – hold your tongue.

PROTEINS, CARBS, FATS AND VITS

Vitamins – the four main ones are called A, B, C and D. Sources of vitamins are cabbage, carrots, oranges, strawberries, blackcurrants, tomatoes and lettuce.

Vitamin A helps to give you a clear healthy skin and good teeth and is necessary for growth. A smiling Legionnaire is a happy Legionnaire. Healthy teeth are essential for grenade work.

Vitamin B helps to give you a good appetite and good digestion and to

Healthy teeth are essential for grenade work.

keep you generally healthy. Vitamin C is most important, for it helps you to resist illness and to give you a clear skin. It is no fun to have man flu in a trench, and a sneezing soldier is a sniper's dream.

In the early campaigns, sailors often suffered from scurvy, a skin disease, because they could not get sufficient fresh foods. Scurvy disappeared when the Britisher Nelson ordered that every sailor should have a daily drink of lime juice, which is rich in Vitamin C. Although he was no friend of the French, he knew his juice and I hear people like his column. I have never read it.

Vitamin D helps in the formation of bones and teeth and it is absorbed into the body from the skin by sunlight.

Proteins or body-building foods – milk, eggs, fish, meat, cheese, peas and beans – help to build up the body and repair wasted tissue. This is obviously vital for wounded Legionnaires.

Carbohydrates or starches and sugars give energy, but too much can make you overweight and harm your teeth and complexion. Carbohydrates are in flour, potatoes sugar, cake, honey, sweets, chocolate, bread and biscuits.

Fats keep the body warm and act as a protective layer under the skin and around the internal organs – margarine, butter and oil (including the oil found in oily fish such as herring) are fats.

Iron and calcium are minerals that keep the blood red and healthy, help to make good bones, teeth and nails and keep you generally in good trim. Kidneys, spinach and liver are my favourite sources of iron – and milk and cheese give us calcium.

"I'LL DO MY SPECIAL ..."

Most men have One Dish that they can make, but a scrumptious Boeuf Stroganoff, or Lamb Vindaloo, or a perfect Beef Wellington often masks the fact that they can't boil an egg with predictable results, and have the toast ready at the same time, or make a basic white sauce.

Cooking for a dinner party is like conducting a symphony orchestra – keeping the main focus in mind but bringing in the supporting players at the right time to make the whole performance a success.

Start simply – when you become familiar with the basic techniques you can progress very quickly. You will start to know by instinct what goes with what. Cooking need not follow the rules – that's the fun of it. Throw open the cupboard and the fridge – what have you got? What's in the fruit bowl? What have you got on the spice rack?

Cooking for a dinner party is like conducting a symphony orchestra. Do choose a cookery book that's in a language you will understand.

CAVEMAN DIET

Serge asked me about the Caveman Diet. Some of my platoon followed this. It was low-carb, non-dairy, gluten-free, additive-free, non-allergic, grain-free, carb-free, low-calorie, low-fat, cholesterol-free, wheat-free, non-radioactive, non-nuclear, dust-free, non-toxic, free-radical-free, eczema-free and sugar-free. But it did have nuts.

Serge asked, if he followed the Caveman Diet, would he turn into a hunter-gatherer? And would he die at thirty, the age cavemen are reputed to have died at? Indeed, if dinosaurs also ate this paleo-diet, is that why they are now extinct? I couldn't answer those questions. But I have to teach Serge the simple rule of moderation in all things, and balance. My favourite caveman recipe is a dairy-free ice cream (but you can use a luxury dairy white vanilla ice cream if you have it to hand) served with a quart of a good ten-year-old Islay malt whisky poured over it.

Alternatively, if you are on the alcohol-free diet, serve the ice cream with the Caveman Chocolate Sauce just before you serve up the ice cream into bowls, particularly if you have just taken it out of the freezer, as it will then be at the right temperature to eat. I have always advised that hunting and gathering is much easier after a helping of ice cream and chocolate sauce.

Before you embark upon this Assault Course, you could try making this – without any basic training.

CAVEMAN CHOCOLATE SAUCE

1 dessertspoon butter (could be dairy-free spread)
1 dessertspoon golden syrup (you can use honey if desperate)
1 dessertspoon cocoa powder

Melt the butter in a saucepan. Add the golden syrup and cocoa powder, and stir over a low heat for a minute, then pour over ice-cream.

When cool, plunge hands into the mixture and make your own cave painting on the kitchen wall. Leave to harden for a thousand years – and hey presto. Food is art!

I happened to be on hand with my instamatic when the Paisley Cave Paintings were discovered. The only existing definitive proof that cavemen ate cupcakes. Sadly, it's now been painted over by an enthusiastic Community Klean operative, clearly "passionate about providing clean and welcoming graffiti-free community areas".

TOOLS AND OPERATIONAL EQUIPMENT

Look in the kitchen to see what you can find. The tools which will lurk on hooks and in drawers and cabinets are not all necessary. Often substitutes can be found, but if you have the right tools it does make the job easier. The palette knife, for example, is very useful for making pastry, removing food from frying pans and bowls, moving biscuits and scones from the baking tray to the cooling tray, and spreading icing on a cake, but if you cannot find one there may be an old table knife that has got thin and bendy, and this will do instead.

The large knife with a pointed end is used for cutting up meat and chopping food like onions and parsley, and you also need a chopping board so that you do not damage your work surface. The board is generally made of hard wood. The small knife is used for preparing vegetables and fruit. It is most useful to have a potato peeler, as you are less likely to peel vegetables and fruit too thickly. Potato peelers can be bought for people who are left-handed. You are sure to find a wooden spoon necessary for mixing and stirring, and there will be a whisk somewhere.

Serge had a close friend, an ex-Royal Gurkha Rifles corporal, who presented him with his kukri. Serge uses it every day.

The kukri is a serious and very effective weapon, and although it looks

like a boomerang, it is not a throwing knife. So any budding kukri knife-thrower should think twice about giving it a hurl.

The kukri is a general-purpose tool sometimes used for woodcutting, and in Nepal is a common agricultural and household implement used for multiple tasks such as chopping firewood, building, digging, skinning and opening tins. And after a good clean, cutting meat and vegetables.

Ladies' kukris are a bit different. They are semi-circular in shape, more like a sickle. And then there is the khurmi, used like a normal kukri for cutting and chopping. There are many kinds of khurmi, with wooden or horn scabbards, and different handles. The khurmi also has a bell so that when it is used the men can know where their womenfolk are in the forest. Every kitchen captain should have one. And put it beside your kukri book.

A whisk is used for beating eggs, cream or sponge mixtures, but again you can often make do with a fork. You will need a grater for grating cheese, making breadcrumbs, grating lemon rind etc., and a lemon squeezer. It is useful to have a sieve or a colander for draining. A colander is like a soldier's helmet which was raised out of the trench to see if the enemy was awake. Cooks like to have sharp knives, but of course take the same care as you would with a bayonet – be careful with them. What we had to do at the front very often was to improvise. Try telling a battle-scarred Legionnaire that the soup isn't ready because we couldn't find the potato peeler …

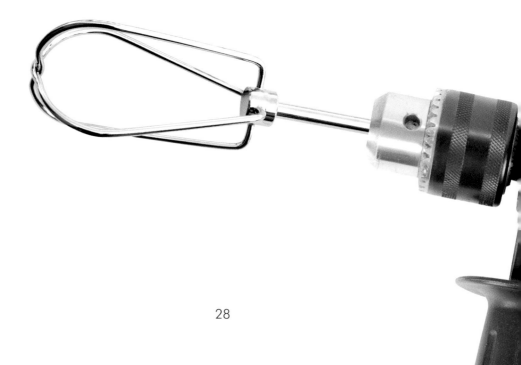

KITCHEN STRATEGY

Before starting a new recipe it is a good idea to go through this routine:

1 Read the recipe through very carefully. You might find it helpful to use a music stand to keep your recipe book on – open at the right place. This will remind you that, like the symphony orchestra conductor, you are in charge at all times. You can keep a baton there too.
2 Collect all the equipment you will need, such as mixing bowl, spoons, saucepan, etc.
3 Collect all the ingredients.
4 Weigh or measure what you need and put the rest away.
5 If you are going to bake, set the oven to the right temperature.
6 Prepare baking tins if you need them.
7 Clear up as you go along.

Loud music will help, so prepare a suitable playlist. For kitchen activities I found a wonderful compilation on Pie Records:
Feels Like I'm In Love – I Knead You
Who's that Lady With My Spam?
Take Me to Paradise When the Cake is Done
If I Can't Have Yours You Can't have Mine
Fire Blanket on the Ground
Hot Love, Gas Mark Six
I'm in the Mood For Icing

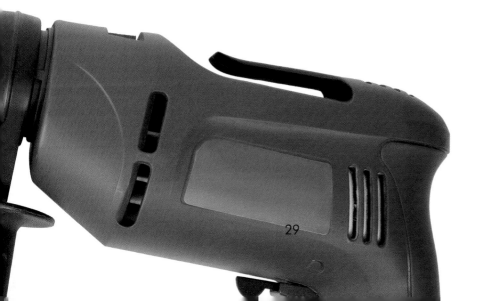

GENERAL COOKING TERMS –
THE LANGUAGE OF THE KITCHEN

Throughout this book you will find certain annoying cookery expressions that you should understand. Here are some of them. We know such terms from our service in the field, but we associate them with violence – beating, for example. The kitchen is no place for violence or harsh interrogation. The kitchen can be your oasis. All that should disturb your concentration is the gentle whistle of your kettle.

To beat. Cake mixtures are beaten with a wooden spoon to incorporate air. Whisking is similar but is generally done with a whisk, especially when you want to beat egg whites stiffly and when making a sponge cake.

To cream. The first process in making a rich fruit cake is to cream the butter and sugar together. It simply means that the two ingredients are beaten until the mixture is soft and fluffy and paler in colour than when you started.

To fold in. When you have a light mixture like stiffly beaten egg white to add to a thicker mixture that has already been beaten you will be told to "fold in the egg white". You use a "cutting" action with a metal spoon, and your aim is to prevent the loss of air.

To rub in. This is the method used for incorporating fat and flour when making pastry and plain cakes. The tips of the fingers are used and the hands should be raised well above the basin to get in as much air as possible. The mixture should look like fine breadcrumbs.

Baking. Cooking in the oven without adding fat, although sometimes the baking tin needs to be greased. Cakes, pastry, biscuits, milk puddings are the most obvious examples.

Roasting. This is also done in the oven but extra fat is used. Joints of meat are generally roasted, and it is a good idea to have a roasting tin with a lid, or cover the tin with a piece of foil. The food may take a little longer to cook but the meat will be kept moist and your oven does not get dirty.

Making exquisite sauces in mountain combat regions is not easy. You try it. For hilltop sauce emergencies – which can be more common than you think – I had Bernard my trusty St Bernard (easy to remember) ready and waiting with his brandy barrel.

Grilling. Small pieces of meat like chops, steaks, sausages, bacon, fish cutlets and small fish like sardines can be cooked under the grill. Look and see where it is on your cooker. The position varies with different kinds of cookers. You need to figure out whether you have a gas cooker or an electric cooker. Gas is good. But the automatic sparker to light it can be annoying when it goes on the blink. There will be a battery to replace somewhere – usually in an inaccessible place at floor level. Beware of lighting a gas oven or grill with a match. There will generally be a build-up of gas when you turn it on, and a small explosion can be anticipated. What we do in France is to make a taper from a newspaper or magazine. This is how Paris Match got its name. Apart from the risk of explosion, gas rings are more controllable: when you turn the heat down, the heat goes down, unlike an electric hob, which takes a while to figure out that you don't want something to boil over.

Frying. This is cooking in fat or oil, although bacon can be fried without adding fat to the pan. A frying pan is used when only a small quantity of fat is needed, as for cooking pancakes or sausages. There is another method, called deep frying, and for this a deeper pan is required and, of course, more fat, and it is the main cause of the outbreak of domestic fires. If your deep pan fryer goes up, before legging it out the door screaming, turn the taps on full and drench a tea towel, or a handy shirt, and drop it flat over the blaze to starve it of oxygen. For best results, remove charred textile remains before resuming the cooking process.

Boiling. This is cooking in boiling liquid, which should be allowed to bubble gently.

Simmering. This is also cooking in water, but you should see only an occasional bubble on the surface of the water.

Steaming. A steamer consists of two pans, one on top of the other. If you have a steamer in your kitchen you will see that the top pan has holes all over the bottom. Water is put into the lower pan and when it boils, the top pan will be full of steam and the food cooks in the steam. It must have a tightly fitting lid so that the steam does not escape. It is an economical way of cooking, as one vegetable could be cooked in the lower pan and another in the top.

Stewing. This is generally a long, slow method of cooking, which is good for the less expensive cuts of meat. Only a little liquid is used and it must simmer very gently. Stews are often cooked in a casserole dish in the oven.

Braising. This is a method of cooking by moist heat and is suitable for the cheaper cuts of meat. The meat is often put on a bed of vegetables and only a very small amount of water is added. The meat can be braised in a stew pan on top of the stove or in a casserole in the oven.

Barding. When meat is wrapped in strips of fat while it cooks, this called barding. Barding keeps meat moist while it cooks, and also imparts flavour. The result is a rich, moist and tender cut of meat. Bacon and fatback are two cuts of meat commonly used for barding.

DEFROSTING FROZEN FOODS

Frozen foods can sometimes be handy but you need to take care. You need to figure out what you've got that can be cooked or baked from frozen, and what needs to be defrosted first. If defrosting is necessary, remember that this takes longer with bigger, denser foods like poultry. There is no real secret about defrosting frozen foods. They just need to be taken out of the freezer and placed in a warmer place. Don't try to speed up the process by placing your frozen food into the oven. Room temperature is all that is necessary, but put it on a sensible dish, to avoid creating alarming puddles for which you might blame the dog.

If you have been given a microwave for Christmas and can still remember where the instruction book is (try down the back of a drawer), have a look. It will have basic directions. Microwave ovens are great for quick defrosting of frozen foods such as meat, poultry, and leftover curries and casseroles. Defrosting in a microwave, straight before you cook the food, reduces the risk of food poisoning from bacteria that can contaminate meat, chicken, fish and other foods thawed over a period of time on your worktop. Take the food out of its packaging and place it in a microwave-safe container or dish. Some retail packaging can melt and contaminate the food. Begin to cook meat, poultry and fish immediately after thawing.

On most microwave ovens, 8 to 10 minutes per 500g on the defrost setting is about the right amount of time needed for most meats.

Your microwave will have a carousel so that the plate will rotate. If you have lost this key accessory or if it has been used as a plant stand, you will need to rotate the food at least six times during the defrost.

For individual pieces that are stuck together, pull the pieces apart and allow space between each. If you are defrosting a large item, such as a duck or a chicken, put it on the carousel on its back, then turn it halfway through.

Time and time again I've asked Serge to defrost that old chest freezer.

SHOPPING AND STORES

Shopping for food is a joy but a busy chef must learn how to find the best ingredients quickly and wisely. Running a busy kitchen means that an old-fashioned shopping list is essential. No time at the Maison de Mince to dash back out to a store because a key item was forgotten. Of course we have our trusted suppliers for regular deliveries, but sometimes if the credit line becomes a little short, I need to make different arrangements, or pop out and pay cash from the tips jar. So my experience of shopping is very useful here to help those of you who are new to the task.

Beware of this internet supermarket shopping. Even if you know exactly what you want, maybe it is some spotty youth who is given your order to pick (and pick he will – probably whilst selecting your peaches), and he is perhaps more concerned about that bit of leg over there than the bit of leg on your list. You can be clever – order the branded goods by phone or by your Blackberry or your Apple, because whilst they might vary in cost the quality is the same. For everything else, best to choose yourself. You will get the freshest lettuce, the glossiest fish and the leanest cuts of meat.

Seasonal foodstuffs do vary a lot in price, and often in quality, so that it is essential to make the choice personally. It is even possible to compromise or substitute items on your list depending on what is available. If the gooseberries don't look great – look at the rhubarb!

If you fancy fish, wait to see what is available at the fishmonger or the fish counter before deciding between cod or mackerel or river cobbler or perhaps you would like to have a nice trout. Same goes for meat – when you see what the butcher has on his tray you might be inspired!

Price changes too according to the season or perhaps it is simply a "special offer" which catches your eye.

From the internet there is the advantage of express home delivery …

There are different grades of bacon, and butter can vary in price according to the country it comes from. Eggs are graded by weight, but the price difference between large, standard, medium and small is worth thinking about.

Then there are the multi-buy offers, and the new products you will come across on your expeditions. Exotic foods from overseas – watermelons, kiwi fruit, vegetables like aubergines. Try them – experiment!

You will learn how to adapt recipes for different ingredients. Nothing is set in stone, although, like ready-mix concrete, which is a hard thing to make, an imbalance in ingredients can lead to disappointment.

The butcher's shop is a daunting place. Meat can all look the same. Good meat-buying skills can be learned. For so many of us, the main dish of a meal is the focus, and for those who are meat eaters or who cater for or entertain meat lovers, some knowledge of meat is very rewarding and in itself is essential dinner party conversation, as is a report on your visit to the farmers' market. Go and look and ask – you might find ostrich steak, perhaps. The seller will know how to cook what they have on display.

Most of the trays in the butcher's shop will be beef. What is beef? Beef is a dead ox, or cow or perhaps a bull, so you can start to understand that a rib of beef might be a joint enough for a small platoon, and a rib of lamb might not give a hungry soldier much to eat.

Lambs frolic in the fields and Mary had one. The doctor was surprised. Lambs can be quite young, or not so young.

A middle-aged lamb becomes a sheep, and in butcher's terms, sheep is mutton, but leg of lamb and shoulder of lamb can often be large – obviously not from a young lamb.

To look at, a piece of beef looks much grainier than a cut of lamb despite the colour seeming the same. Really young lamb is a good deal paler and not rough in texture.

Which brings me to pork! The colour of pork can be anything between pink and a creamy white, and beware of fatty pork.

Veal is "calf" – the young version of beef, and it is a much softer pink than lamb but much rosier in colour than pork.

Your butcher is an ally, not an enemy. His skill is immense. He has bigger knives and choppers than you and he can bone pieces of meat to make them easier to carve at the table – particularly ribs of beef, breast of veal or lamb, shoulder of lamb, or loin of veal.

What you need to think about is if there is bone included in what you buy – the weight won't give you the amount you hoped for once the bone is discarded. Is this kind of meat going to shrink when cooked?

Some cuts of meat are easier to cook than others – so you need to think about the whole meal and how much attention it will take when you decide what your main dish will be. (I think this is the best advice I can give. Focus on one part of the meal and get it right. If you are aiming for a three courser, prepare something in advance for the starter and for the dessert, so you are not spinning all sorts of plates and pots at the same time.)

Back to the shopping. In price terms, smaller, younger animals will cost more than their older brothers and sisters. Some parts of the carcass are dearer than others – rear end will cost more than front end, and smaller, more easily cooked pieces (like fillet) will cost more than other cuts.

And never forget the mince. I am the Prince of Mince. Learn about mince. Be aware of mince. Beef mince ground for you by your butcher is magical, but you can mince scraps and leftovers from your joint, and meat dumplings or shepherd's pie can be heaven. Always count the pennies. Have a sharp eye for a bargain. Beware of having to cook a cheap cut of meat with expensive ingredients – mushrooms, peppers, perhaps with cream or fruit.

WEIGHING AND MEASURING

As we make progress, you will realise that it is important to have the right amount of each ingredient to get good results every time. We know this from our work with explosives and concrete.

It is just the same idea.

However, do not worry if you have no scales; you can manage very well with spoons and cups. A tablespoon or teaspoon is the best thing to use for measuring small quantities of dry goods like flour and sugar. You will probably find several in the kitchen cupboard; look at them carefully and you will no doubt see that they vary a little in size. You could invest in a set of measuring spoons. These are not expensive to buy and are very useful if you have no scales. A level spoonful is filled level with the edge of the spoon. Put the spoon into the flour or whatever it is you want to measure and draw a flat knife across the top. A rounded spoonful means there should be as much above the bowl of the spoon as below. A heaped spoonful means there is as much in the spoon as it will hold. The rounded and heaped spoonful cannot be as accurate as a level spoonful. It is easy to make a mistake with a rounded spoonful, and a heaped one is rather difficult to handle.

In a recipe you will often be asked to add a "pinch" of salt. This means as much as you can pick up between your thumb and first finger.

BASIC TRAINING

BUTTERED TOAST

Toast is bread which has been exposed to a dry heat. This browning reaction is known as the Maillard reaction, named after the French chemist, Monsieur Louis-Camille Maillard, who identified it. He didn't invent it, of course – the history of toast goes back to the early Neolithic cooks, who had to invent bread first. Toasting warms the bread and makes it firmer, so that it can be a vehicle for tasty toppings. Toasting is also a good way of disguising stale bread.

The Romans liked a bit of toast. In fact all through history, toast has had its place. Today, the main method of making toast is with an electric toaster. The first one was invented in 1893 by Crompton & Co. and toasted one side of the bread at a time. The pop-up toaster was invented in 1919.

For best results, place pre-sliced bread into the opening at the top of the toaster. Look for a lever which allows the bread to drop into the body of the machine. There will be different settings which control how long the bread is exposed to the dry heat. The toast is done when it pops up.

If smoke begins to fill the kitchen, and the smoke alarm starts to scream, this probably means that the bread has become jammed (that is, trapped in the mechanism, rather than been liberally covered with preserves). Switch off the toaster and let it cool before attempting to clear the jam.

You can also toast bread under a grill, but you need to watch closely and turn the bread once one side is done to your liking.

Toast is most commonly enjoyed by spreading butter over it with a knife using a left-to-right, right-to-left technique, to achieve an even coating. Secondary coatings such as jam, honey etc. can be applied, and firm favourites with advanced cooks are baked beans on toast and scrambled eggs or fried eggs on toast.

LEFT: Clockwise from the top, "blue" toast (i.e. bread), medium-rare, medium and well-done

COOKING WITH EGGS

You know that eggs contain protein because I told you. Eggs can be the main part of a meal and are used in all kinds of cakes and puddings. Many times we raided the henhouses near our front line to help us survive. The hens, however, do not date-stamp their offering – and in a war zone we need to check if they are fresh. How to do this? Put the egg in water – a few inches will do. If it sinks and lies on its side, it is a fresh egg. If it sinks but sits on its end, it is not so fresh, but OK. If it floats, use it as ammunition and sling it.

If you hear a tapping noise and the eggshell begins to crack, the egg is probably past its best.

The easiest way to break an egg is to hold it in your left hand and tap the shell lightly with a knife. Then put your thumbs into the crack and carefully break the shell apart. When you become cavalier enough to crack an egg on the side of a frying pan and open it with the same hand, and drop it perfectly to cook, you will know that you have earned some respect. This requires the same dexterity as a Legionnaire who can roll a cigarette with one hand. If you are using several eggs for cooking, be sure to break each egg separately into a small basin or cup to make sure it is fresh before adding to the mixture.

If the white is to be separated from the yolk, slide the yolk carefully from one half of the shell to the other, allowing the white to fall into the basin below. When you have to beat egg whites stiffly, take the eggs from the fridge about an hour before you need them, as the white will beat up more easily if it is not too cold. A pinch of salt also helps.

TO BOIL EGGS

There are two methods. Try both to see which you prefer.

For the first method, lower the eggs on a tablespoon carefully into a pan of boiling water. See that you have enough water to cover the eggs. Allow 4 minutes for a soft-boiled egg, 5 minutes if you like it a little firmer, and 10 minutes for hard-boiled.

The second method is to put the eggs into cold water and when the water boils, allow 3 minutes for a soft-boiled egg, 4 minutes for a firmer egg and 10 minutes for hard-boiled. Some people think the egg white is a little lighter if this method is used.

TO FRY EGGS

You need a frying pan and a small amount of butter or oil. If you are frying bacon with the eggs, the bacon should be cooked first and kept hot and you will probably find there is enough fat left in the pan to cook the eggs. If not, put a small knob of butter or a little oil into the pan and heat it. Break the egg into a saucer or a cup and slide it carefully into the hot fat, reduce the heat and cook the egg slowly. Spoon a little of the fat over the egg yolk while it is cooking. The egg will take only 2 to 3 minutes to cook. If you are frying more than one egg, put the first into the pan and leave it until the white just begins to set before adding the second. When the first egg is cooked, take it out of the pan carefully with a fish slice with a thin metal edge. There are many ways of serving fried eggs other than with bacon. You can make a good meal by putting a fried egg on baked beans on toast.

You will think of other ideas.

TO SCRAMBLE EGGS

Scrambled eggs are good to make because there are so many ways of serving them – perhaps with smoked salmon – and so many extra things you can add. If you are just cooking for yourself, two eggs may be enough, it depends how hungry you are. Allow 1 tablespoon of milk to each egg.

Break the eggs into a basin and beat lightly with a fork, just enough to mix the yolk and white together. Add the milk and do not forget to add a pinch of salt and a shake of pepper.

Melt a little butter in a small pan – you will need about 15g for each egg – and stir over a low heat with a wooden spoon until the mixture begins to thicken, then take it off the heat and it will finish cooking in the saucepan. If you cook it too much it will become dry and crumbly, and

You can also cook bacon on an iron, and steam irons can be especially useful.

remember the heat must be low otherwise it will go watery.

Scrambled egg is fantastic served on hot buttered toast.

Think of things which could be added to the beaten egg before it is cooked. A few suggestions are chopped cooked sausage, chopped ham, peeled sliced tomatoes or chopped parsley.

TO POACH EGGS

For the beginner this is perhaps the most difficult way of cooking eggs, so if you get a good result first time you can be proud of yourself. Some people have a proper egg poacher, but her day off is a Thursday, so we need to know what to do.

It is easy to overcook the egg, so try doing it this way. Use a shallow pan or a frying pan and half fill it with water. Add a pinch of salt and heat the water to boiling point. Now put a plain round metal or ceramic biscuit cutter in the pan to keep the egg a good shape.

Break the egg into a cup and slide it carefully into the cutter. Turn the heat down a little and leave for about 4 minutes, when the egg should be lightly set. Remove the cutter and, using a fish slice or a perforated spoon, remove the egg from the pan. If you cannot find a cutter, then wait until the water is boiling, stir it rapidly and slide the egg into the middle of the swirl. Reduce the heat at once.

Another way: get some microwaveable clingfilm and make a pouch in a teacup, as if lining the cup. Break the egg into it, close the film like a bag and drop it into the water. When it is cooked, you can fish it out and unwrap your parcel, revealing a perfect poached egg.

Poached eggs can be served on toast, or on cooked spinach or smoked haddock.

TO MAKE AN OMELETTE

This is not difficult but it does need a little practice. If you are not successful the first time, try again. There is no need to waste the egg mixture – it will taste quite good even if it does not look perfect. If all goes wrong when

preparing the romantic omelette dinner, the best course is to take romantic action – turn off the lights and light a candle – just enough light to identify that there is food on the plate, but not enough to expose it to criticism.

You need two large or three small eggs to make an omelette big enough for one person. You also need a small frying pan or, better still, a pan kept for cooking only omelettes and pancakes. Choose a thick pan with a smooth surface.

You can make a plain or filled omelette. The filling can be cooked mushrooms, cooked tomatoes, chopped ham, cheese, etc., but prepare this before cooking the eggs, as the omelette must be served as soon as it is cooked.

1   Break the eggs into a bowl, add a pinch of salt, a shake of pepper and 2 tablespoons water or milk.
2   Beat lightly with a fork as you did for scrambled eggs.
3   Heat 30g butter in the pan, pour in the egg mixture, stir lightly with a fork and leave it for just about 30 seconds, then tilt the pan slightly and, using a fork, move the mixture away from the edge so that the uncooked egg runs underneath.
4   Cook for about 2 minutes, place any filling on one half of the surface, then slip a palette knife under one side of the omelette, tilt the pan and fold the omelette over.
5   Holding the warm serving plate in your left hand and the pan in your right, tip the folded omelette out on to the plate. (Or the other way around if you are left-handed.)

EGGY BREAD

When I first opened the Maison de Mince for breakfast custom, I discovered that the popular request "Gonnae make us eggy bread mister" was an appeal for French toast.

Now that you are a master egg-handler, you are up to this task. Make up an egg mixture – say three eggs and three dessertspoons of milk and beat it. Heat the frying pan with a little butter – just a coating, plunge a slice of bread into the mixture – in and out so you don't end up with a soggy mass, and place it on the pan. Brown one side, flip it over with a fish slice and brown the other. You can add cinnamon to your mix, and serve with sugar, butter, fruit, syrup or jam, but best is North American style – with maple syrup and with bacon on the side.

MAKING A WHITE SAUCE

A basic white sauce, or bechamel, is a key basic "starter" sauce for many recipes. It's a base for macaroni cheese, an important element of moussaka, and the kicking-off point for scores of other sauces.

A good thick white sauce also can hide a multitude of sins. Women have been disguising their culinary disasters for hundreds of years with white sauce. If you are masking a real corker, take their mind off it by stirring a tablespoon of hot mustard into a basic white sauce.

You will need:
>   30g butter,
>   30g plain flour
>   300ml milk, or vegetable stock
>   Salt and pepper

Method:
1   Heat the butter in a small saucepan.
2   Remove it from the heat, add the flour and stir it well in with a wooden spoon. This mixture of fat and flour is called a "roux", which you pronounce "roo".
3   Put the pan back over a low heat and cook for about 2 minutes, stirring all the time.
4   Take the pan off the heat again and gradually add the liquid, stirring in a little at a time so that the mixture is quite smooth. Add a pinch of salt and a shake of pepper.
5   Return the pan to the heat and stir all the time until the sauce boils and thickens. Reduce the heat and let the sauce simmer for 2 minutes. Taste it to see if there is enough seasoning.

SAUCES THAT CAN BE MADE FROM WHITE SAUCE

Cheese. Add 6–8 level tablespoons of grated cheese and stir until melted.
Hard-boiled egg. Add one or two chopped hard-boiled eggs. This is often served with chicken or fish.
Parsley. Add 2 level tablespoons of finely chopped parsley and serve with vegetables, fish or boiled bacon.
Anchovy. Add half a teaspoon of anchovy essence and be careful not to add too much salt. This is often served with fish.
Mustard. Add 1 tablespoon of mustard (or add to taste) to white sauce.

HOW TO MAKE A BATTER

Eggs are also used for making batters, both sweet and savoury. You may have tasted Yorkshire pudding, which is made with a batter, and it can also be used to make a complete dish like Toad in the Hole (page 134). Pancakes are also made from batter. By using less than the usual amount of milk and making the batter thicker, you can make a batter for coating fish, etc., for frying.

To make a batter you will need:
>   120g plain flour
>   A pinch of salt
>   1 egg
>   1 litre milk (or milk and water mixed)

Method:
1   Sieve the flour and salt into a fairly large basin and make a hole in the centre of the flour.
2   Break the egg into a cup to be sure it is fresh and drop it into the hole. Add about a quarter of the milk and stir with a wooden spoon until well mixed. Beat hard until the batter is smooth.
3   Add half of the remaining milk and continue to beat well, then add the rest of the milk, give it a final beat and put aside in a cool place until you need it.

YORKSHIRE PUDDING

Use the above batter to make Yorkshire pudding.

In Yorkshire, many people have Yorkshire pudding as a separate course before the meat, and they think it is best to use half milk and half water to make the batter. When you do it, you can try both ways and see if you agree. The secret of making a good batter is to beat plenty of air into it and to let it stand in a cool place for an hour or so before cooking. If you beat the batter properly, it makes a noise like galloping horses coming towards you. Is that a light at the end of the tunnel or a train coming?

Method:

1   Preheat the oven to 200°C.
2   Use a large roasting tin, or individual patty tins. Add cooking fat (beef dripping is traditional) to the tin and place in the oven, one thrid from the top, to heat.
3   When you see a heat haze above the fat remove from oven and pour in the batter.
4   Place back on the same shelf and cook for approximately 30 minutes.

If you make Yorkshire pudding outside Yorkshire you may need to call it something else soon. Irate pudding makers are campaigning for European protection so only puddings made in Yorkshire can be true Yorkshire ones. I might have to rename my Sunday roast thus: Roast Beef with Yorkshire-style Paisley-made Savoury Batter Puddings. Catchy.

PANCAKES

Pancake Day is also known as Shrove Tuesday and celebrates the start of the celebration of Lent where some Christians give up something or fast for 40 days to empathise with Jesus when he was sent into the wilderness for 40 days and nights and tempted by the Devil … so the day before, folk would use up all the food items in the home such as sugar, butter, milk and eggs so they were not wasted. I like to add gin to that list.

Ingredients:
>   300ml batter (page 50)
>   Cooking fat or oil
>   Sugar
>   1 lemon or orange, or jam
>   (Have ready a piece of
>   greaseproof or kitchen paper
>   sprinkled with sugar.)

Method:

1   Heat about 15g cooking fat or 1 tablespoon oil in a small frying pan. Watch it carefully until you see a very faint haze rising.

2   Pour in a very little batter, only enough to give a paper-thin layer in the pan. Cook for 2 minutes, then turn the pancake over and cook the other side for 2 minutes. Until you are more experienced, turn the pancake with a palette knife or fish slice.

3   Turn the pancake out on to sugared paper, sprinkle with more sugar, squeeze some orange or lemon juice over or put a spoonful of jam on top, then roll it up.

4   Put it on to a hot plate and keep it hot in the oven or over a pan of hot water while you make the rest of the pancakes.

5   This quantity of batter will make ten to twelve pancakes if you make them thin. You will probably have to add a little fat or oil for each pancake, but make sure it is hot each time. If the pancakes are to be kept hot for any length of time, do not sprinkle them with the fruit juice. Serve slices of orange or lemon separately.

TO TOSS A PANCAKE

This is not really difficult but it does need a little practice. First be quite sure that the pancake is not sticking to the pan. Shake the pan to be certain. Hold the pan securely in your right hand. Tilt the pan downwards a little, then give a sharp upward flick and the pancake should fall back in the pan with the cooked side uppermost. You could practise this with an empty pan. When you try this for the first time, put a piece of clean paper on the floor – just in case of accidents. And if you have a central kitchen light, move to one side of it.

COOKING BREAKFAST

A Legionnaire will never miss le petit dejeuner. Breakfast is very important. It may be his last meal for many hours.

You have read about frying, and got to grips with Eggy Bread, so now you can cook a proper breakfast. There are lots of things to choose from, but try this Legion favourite first: bacon with tomatoes and fried bread. If you are, sadly, cooking only for yourself, you will need:

> 1–2 rashers of bacon
> 1 tomato
> Salt and pepper
> 1 slice of bread

Method:

1   Cut the rind off the bacon with a pair of kitchen scissors or your sharp knife, kukri or bayonet.
2   Cut the tomato in half and sprinkle with salt and pepper.
3   Put the bacon and the rind into a frying pan. There is no need to add fat, as some will run from the bacon, and the rind (added to the pan, but to be discarded later) will give a little extra.
4   Turn on the heat and if the rashers are thin they will cook in about 2 minutes. You can easily tell by the colour of the fat – it will look golden and not transparent as it did before cooking.
5   When it is nearly done, put in the tomato halves and cook for about one minute.
6   Put the bacon and tomatoes on a hot plate and keep hot.
7   Put the bread into the pan and cook for about one minute then turn it over and cook the other side. It should be crisp and brown. Put the bread on the plate with the bacon – and there is the main course of your breakfast. You will of course have discarded the bacon rind. If you start with fruit juice or cereal and finish with toast and marmalade or honey, you will have had a good nourishing meal and have made a sensible start to the day.

BOILING, SIMMERING AND POACHING

The easiest way to cook just about anything is to put it in water and heat it up. Please refer to the photograph opposite for one way to do this.

In 1531 Henry VIII of England passed an Act, allowing boiling as a form of capital punishment – and something we cooks should bear in mind is that a cook named Richard Roose, who poisoned several unfortunates, was the first to be boiled alive under this Act.

To boil: pour water into a saucepan, put it on the hob and heat it until you can see bubbles rising to the surface. Wait until you have an even boil, with bubbles the size of peas, all across the surface, then place in the food. You can boil a kettle to make the process quicker. When you place in the food, the boil will reduce initially – wait until it is back as before, then reduce the heat slightly so that there is a continuous bubbling movement. Simmering and poaching is cooking like this, just below boiling point. Fierce boiling is only needed to reduce liquid in a sauce, for example.

Count the cooking time from the point that the boil resumes after the food is in the water.

TEA

You can practice "boiling" by making a pot of tea :
1   Boil the water in a whistling kettle (so that you can hear above your loud kitchen playlist).
2   As the water begins to boil, remove your whistling kettle from the heat.
3   Pour a small amount of water into your teapot. This will "warm" the pot. Discard the water.
4   Pour the remainder of boiling water into the teapot.
5   Add tea to the teapot. If you're using tea bags, add four bags for every six cups of tea. If you're using leaves, pack them into a tea ball. (Note: Tea balls can only be filled halfway. Overpacking a tea ball may cause it to explode. Not a dangerous explosion, but irritating nevertheless.)
6   Watch the clock. Most types of tea take 3–5 minutes.
7   Remove tea bags and balls, otherwise you will end up with a second cup with the consistency and taste of an Irish stew.

COOKING WITH VEGETABLES

Before learning how to cook vegetables you should know how to buy them. Vegetables, especially green ones, contain valuable vitamins but they lose some of these when they are stale or overcooked. Vegetables can be divided roughly into three groups:

Root vegetables, like potatoes and carrots. We'll include onions here because they grow under the ground but an onion is a bulb.

Green vegetables, like cabbage, sprouts and spinach.

Pulses, which can be fresh, like peas, broad beans and runner beans, or dried, like haricot beans, lentils and dried peas.

Root vegetables should be firm and have no blemishes. A carrot that you can tie a knot in is probably past its best.

Green vegetables should be a fresh colour and firm. Do not buy them if the leaves look yellow and tired.

Peas and beans should be firm and green. Avoid runner beans that are very big and hard. Young ones snap easily.

TO COOK ROOT VEGETABLES

First of all wash them well in plenty of cold water.

Then peel thinly or scrape according to the vegetable – old potatoes and carrots are peeled and new ones scraped.

Root vegetables are usually boiled, but there are other methods of cooking, as you will see later.

For each 450g of prepared vegetables you will need about 850ml to 1 litre of water.

Bring the water to boiling point and add 1 level teaspoon of salt. Put in the vegetables, cover with the lid of the pan and boil gently until the vegetables are tender. The time varies according to the age and size of the vegetable, but as a rough guide, carrots take about 20 minutes. Be careful not to overcook.

Test them by pricking with a skewer or the tip of a knife. They should be tender but not too soft.

Drain off as much of the water as you possibly can, then put a knob of butter into the saucepan.

Put the pan back over a low heat for a few minutes to dry off the vegetables.

Serve in a warmed vegetable dish with a little chopped parsley on top. This improves the appearance and adds a little Vitamin C.

BOILED POTATOES

The best way to boil potatoes is in their skins and the best news is that you don't need to peel them – just give them a good wash, then cover them with boiling water and boil for about 20 minutes. A gentle boil will give the best results – they will be evenly cooked from the outside to the centre. Bigger potatoes will need a few minutes longer, as will "new" potatoes. To test when they are ready, use a fork to make sure the potato is soft all the way through. If you can't make up your mind, remove one with a spoon and cut it in half and taste it. Remove the pan from the heat and drain by holding the lid just to one side. Serve with butter, sprinkled with chopped parsley.

To peel potatoes, use a proper peeler, as a knife can take off too much (unless you want to have a snack of deep-fried potato skins with melted cheese later on). Cut the potatoes into even-sized pieces and cover with boiling water. Small pieces will take less time than larger pieces – but beware of making them too small or they can turn to mush. About 20 minutes on a gentle boil should do the trick.

SPECIAL MASH

Another opportunity to present something so simple but memorable is to create your own signature mashed potato.

Having added milk and butter, and some salt and pepper, to your boiled potatoes and pulverised them into the smoothest mash ever, that's not made up of powder out of a packet, try putting some texture back in.

Fried onions. Thinly sliced, gently fried until they are golden brown, and mixed into your mash.

Cabbage. Cut into ribbons, steamed and stirred in.

Hot creamy mash. Gently fry 2 teaspoons of mustard seeds with about a teaspoon of chopped green chilli until the mustard seeds pop, then stir into two dollops of crème fraîche, and blend into the mash.

Garlic mash. Finely chop 3 or 4 cloves. Melt 25g butter with the chopped garlic and heat gently over the lowest setting you can use, for about 20 minutes. Make sure the garlic does not get brown. Add the butter and garlic to the mash, along with freshly ground black pepper and a handful of grated cheese and mix it all in.

Classic mash trio. Try a blend of equal parts potato, turnip and carrot well mashed with a few grinds of black pepper.

Mustard is great in mash, but don't go over the top. Some English mustard – a teaspoon mixed into enough mash for four people – gives mash an edge.

Finely grated cheese. Well mixed-in, plus a little sprinkled on top, and put the dish under the grill for a few minutes – wonderful!

TO COOK GREEN VEGETABLES

CABBAGE AND GREENS

Remove any withered leaves and wash in cold water. Cut into shreds with a sharp knife. For each 450g of prepared vegetables, have only about 4–5cm of water in the pan. Bring the water to the boil and add 1 level teaspoon of salt. Add the greens a handful at a time and let the water come to the boil again before adding the next handful. Put the lid on the pan and boil fairly quickly for 5 to 7 minutes. Strain as for root vegetables, but be particularly careful to press out all the water.

CAULIFLOWER

This can be cooked whole or divided into florets. Allow 15 minutes for a small whole cauliflower and 8–10 minutes if cut up.

SPINACH

The favourite of Popeye the Sailor Man. After washing well in several changes of water, put it into the pan without any extra water and sprinkle a little salt between each layer. Cover tightly with the lid of the pan and cook for 12–15 minutes. Drain very carefully.

THE JOY OF SPROUTS

Brussels sprouts are part of the Brassica family of vegetables, which includes cabbage, broccoli and kale. In a recent survey Brussels sprouts were declared the most hated vegetable in Britain. How can this be?

We should glory in sprouts. Sprouts, glorious sprouts! We should forgive the Belgians – and allow them to eat boudin sausage in appreciation of sprouts. They contain sinigrin, a compound which, according to some boffins, could prevent colon cancer. One helping of Brussels sprouts contains Vitamin A and beta carotene, contains only sixty calories, and has 80 per cent of the recommended daily allowance of Vitamin C. Trim and wash them well, cut a cross at the bottom of each and cook as for cabbage, allowing 7–10 minutes.

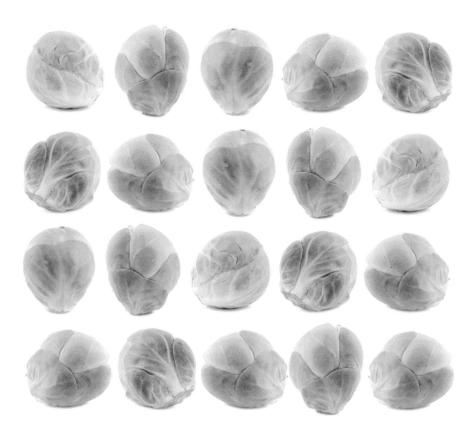

STEAMING VEGETABLES

I came late to steaming because we did not have much advanced equipment at the front. It is a magnificent way to cook most vegetables. It is gentle, the vegetables keep their shape and form, their texture and colour, but most important I think is the flavour they keep. Nutrition and goodness are not lost to the surging waters of the boiling pot. Steaming is also very easy.

A steamer has a base pan and one or more pans stacked on top, with holes in the bases of the inner pans and, importantly, a lid. So you can do different vegetables one on top of the other and the steam goes through them all. If you are a very tall chef, you can have more, but you need to adjust the steaming times at the top as the steam is less steamy.

Ensure the water in the base pan does not touch the bottom of the steamer basket. Bring the water to the boil before adding the vegetables to the basket. Cover and cook.

Make sure the water doesn't boil away. Add more boiling water from your whistling kettle to the pan when it is needed.

EXAMPLES OF VEGETABLE STEAMING TIMES

Artichokes, medium, 40 minutes
Asparagus, thin spears, 4 minutes; thick spears, 6 minutes
Broccoli, florets, 5 minutes; spears, 5 minutes
Brussels sprouts, 10 minutes
Cabbage, cut in pieces, 6 minutes
Carrots, cut about 5mm thick, 8 minutes
Cauliflower, head, 15 minutes; florets, 5 minutes
Corn on the cob, 5 minutes
Courgettes, 5mm slices, 6 minutes
Green beans, 5 minutes
Kale, 10 minutes
Parsnips, 3–4cm pieces, 10 minutes
Peas, 3 minutes
Potatoes, new, 12 minutes; 5cm pieces, 15 minutes
Spinach, 5 minutes
Sweet potatoes, whole, 20 minutes; 2–3cm pieces,
    10 minutes

COOKING VEGETABLES IN THE OVEN

Vegetables can also be cooked in the oven. Carrots, for example, are excellent this way. Choose a casserole with a tight-fitting lid. Put in about 30g of butter or oil, a pinch of salt and about 1 tablespoon of water. Add thinly sliced carrots, put on the lid and cook in a fairly hot oven, 190°C, gas mark 5, for about 40 minutes.

Potatoes can be baked in their jackets in the oven. Scrub the skins well, brush them with a little oil, then put them on a baking tray or roasting tin and bake in a fairly hot oven, 190°C, gas mark 5, for an hour or more, depending on the size. Test them with a sharp knife to make sure they are soft all the way through. Split open their skins as soon as you take them out of the oven, and mash a little butter into them, along with some salt and pepper.

Many vegetables are improved if they are served with a sauce. It can be a plain white sauce, or a parsley or cheese sauce (see page 49). Obviously, the sauce will improve the food value of the vegetable. In fact, cauliflower served with a cheese sauce makes a complete supper or light lunch dish (see page 65).

Other vegetables improved with a sauce are leeks, celery, chicory, beetroot, and broad beans, as well as dried haricot or butter beans.

The most wonderful onions you will ever taste can be made without tears!

Onions have their own skins – don't do anything to them, just put them in the oven to bake at 170°C, gas mark 3, for about an hour. The skin acts like a little pressure cooker. Serve in a dish straight from the oven and let your guests get at them!

SIZE MATTERS

Remember The Borrowers? Tiny people who lived in big people's houses and borrowed things to survive while keeping their existence secret?

Chefs far and wide are looking at Borrowers-sized vegetables as the new "cuisine de curiosité". Growers are crowding vegetables, stunting growth and plucking miniature carrots, cabbages and courgettes after two weeks growth.

Micro-greens indeed! Have they not heard of sprouts and peas?

It seems that one end of the country is growing giant marrows and leeks to win prizes, while the other is farming in Legoland with Mrs Tittlemouse and Hunca Munca.

It doesn't seem very "green" not to let a seed be efficient and grow to its potential – and by the time you've peeled a dwarf carrot there'll be nothing left!

What would be served with micro-veg? Micro-chips? Micro-fish?

FROZEN VEGETABLES

Look in the frozen food cabinets and you will see a large variety of frozen vegetables. Make a list of them so that you can refer to it when you come to prepare menus.

MAKING CAULIFLOWER CHEESE

Get cauliflower – add cheese. It's a little bit more involved than that but it's not hard. Now that you have learned how to cook cauliflower and make a white sauce, you can prepare this dish.

Ingredients:

    1 cauliflower
    Salt
    300ml cheese sauce (see page 49 for White
    Sauce)
    A little extra grated cheese
    1 level tablespoon breadcrumbs
    15g butter

Method:

1. Wash the cauliflower and cut it into florets. (When you get more experienced you can cook it whole.)
2. Remove some of the hard white stalk but some of the tender green leaf can be cooked with the cauliflower.
3. Boil about 250ml of water, add half a level teaspoon of salt and put in the cauliflower. Put on the lid and cook for about 10 minutes.
4. While the cauliflower is cooking you can make the sauce.
5. Test the cauliflower with a skewer or fork to make sure it is just tender, drain off the water and put the cauliflower into an ovenproof dish. If you have some individual ovenproof dishes, you could serve individual portions.
6. Pour the sauce over the cauliflower, sprinkle with a little extra cheese and the breadcrumbs, and dot with butter.
7. Put the dish under a hot grill for a few minutes to brown the top or, if you have the oven in use, you can brown the top in the oven, but obviously it would not be worth lighting the oven specially. You can serve grilled tomatoes with this dish and mashed or boiled potatoes.

This will be enough for four people. You can make some interesting variations on this dish. Instead of making a cheese sauce, pour a small tin of condensed tomato or mushroom soup over the cooked cauliflower and heat it through in the oven.

TO COOK BEANS AND PULSES

Be aware that dried beans and pulses can cause copius amounts of flatulent intestinal gas. Other flatulence foods include onions, garlic, potatoes, artichokes, leeks, turnips, radishes, cauliflower, broccoli and cabbage. Brussels sprouts and other brassicas are particularly pungent. Everything in moderation. Including flatulence.

Some spices can help – I mean in the food, not to mask dining room odours. Cumin, coriander and caraway seeds – turmeric too, and if you have any Japanese seaweed, that's good too. At least it will take your mind off it.

Fresh beans and peas. Peas and broad beans are removed from the pods, but if broad beans are very young they can be prepared like runner beans. For these, cut off the ends and stringy sides and cut into slices. French

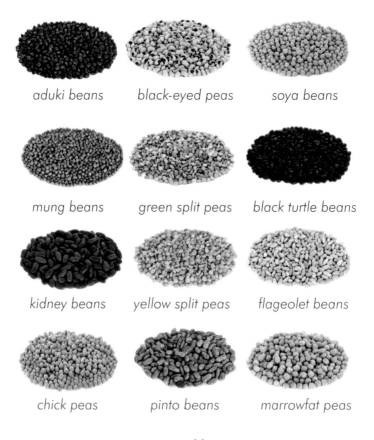

aduki beans   black-eyed peas   soya beans

mung beans   green split peas   black turtle beans

kidney beans   yellow split peas   flageolet beans

chick peas   pinto beans   marrowfat peas

beans are generally cooked whole. All these are cooked as for green vegetables.

Dried pulses. Haricot beans, lentils, etc., are best soaked overnight, although split red lentils do not require soaking before they are cooked.

1 For 120g beans allow 600ml of boiling water.
2 Put the dried beans in a saucepan, pour on the water and leave until the next day. Then bring the water to the boil, add 1 level teaspoon of salt, cover with a lid and simmer gently.
3 Haricot beans will take about 2 hours, lentils and peas about 1 hour.
4 Strain and serve with a little butter or a sauce.

The next time you go into a supermarket look and see what a range of dried vegetables there is. You can buy dried peas and beans that do not need soaking because they are frozen by a special method before being dried. You will see on the packet AFD, which means Accelerated Freeze-Dried. On the packet you will find clear directions for cooking.

LENTILS

There is a whole world of lentils to discover. There must be more than a hundred varieties of lentils to explore – brown, pink, yellow, green, black – not just the ordinary little red lentils.

Massimo was with us in the Legion. He said that in Italy, it is lucky to eat lentils on New Year's Day. The rest of the platoon didn't agree. So it turned out not to be such a lucky day for Massimo after all.

The best lentils are the French puy lentils, once grown only in France, but now also cultivated more widely. Although grey-green in colour, they are sometimes called blue lentils. They come with their skins on and don't change colour when they are cooked.

Lentils absorb any cooking liquid – red wine, or vegetable or chicken stock – and seasoning. Try cinnamon, cloves, garlic, ginger, cardamom, fennel, thyme, tarragon, bay or coriander, for a lentil experience.

green lentils   *puy lentils*   *red lentils*

SALAD

Salad is hugely underrated, and a fantastic opportunity to be creative with leaves. "Wow!" you are thinking, "I'm so uncreative when it comes to leaves."

Think beyond basic lettuce and the usual, predictable inclusions and embark on a whole new adventure of chopping, combining, slicing, dicing and tossing. Enter also the world of dips – not a ride at Euro Disney – dishes accompanied by cottage cheese, hummus, taramasalata and yoghurts.

A great investment is a mighty salad bowl and a manly pair of salad servers or tongs. "And tongs to you too," you may well say, but read on.

Mix your leaves – iceberg, or Little Gem lettuce, rocket, watercress, spinach – and some beansprouts will add extra texture.

Delight your guests by letting them help themselves, thereby joining in the creative salad process. Put salad components out in small dishes with spoons, and whisk them to the table on trays overflowing with choice for your guests. Who knew salad could be so dramatic?

Remember Cole's Law: Thinly sliced cabbage.

I just worry that one day a scientist will discover that salad is fattening after all and that's why I can't shift my love handles.

Nuts – cashews, monkey nuts (shelled), pistachios
Walnuts – drizzled in runny honey
Seeds – sesame seeds and sunflower seeds
Cheeses – cheddar or blue cheese, and cheeses that grate or crumble
Olives
Dates and Raisins
Peppers
Carrots – grated, or kept as crunchy sticks
Cucumber – sliced or cut into sticks
Croutons – cut the crusts off toast and cut into small cubes the size of sweetcorn.
Crispy bacon – cooled and chopped
Onion – finely chopped onion, but don't overdo it (whole spring onions are a better option in take-it-or-leave-it selections)

Tomatoes – beef tomatoes sliced; small vine tomatoes whole
Red cabbage – chopped or shredded
Radishes
Pickled Beetroot – sliced or grated (but add as a finishing touch, otherwise everything will take on a purple/pinkish colour)
Cauliflower florets
Peas
Grapes, orange segments, lemon slices, apricots, peaches, apple slices
Melon – (small pieces or balls) sprinkled with ground ginger

Meaty additions will turn your salad into a substantial meal –
Tuna or **salmon** or **anchovies**
Chicken or **turkey** or **duck breast**
Ham
Sausage slices and **bacon** or **meatballs**
Don't forget the wonderful **salamis** and **chorizos**
Eggs – hard-boiled and sliced, or warm poached eggs

Here are some other ideas:

A bit on the side – mango chutney, mayonnaise, honey mustard vinaigrette.

Use smaller dishes – with textures and tastes combined – don't be restricted to making a salad in one bowl.

Couscous – a great vehicle to carry chopped fruit.

Yoghurt – carries chopped guavas, apricots or peaches.

Boiled rice – cooked rice, immediately rinsed in cold water and cooled (this is important – cooked rice left too long at room temperature can give you food poisoning), mixed with cooked and cooled mushrooms chopped and stirred in, maybe with some diced red, yellow and green peppers, and bacon bits.

Fruit – There is no shame in using tinned fruits for some of these bits on the side – in fact, I think that when you are combining guavas, apricots, prunes or peaches with yoghurts, the tinned varieties work very well indeed.

COBB SALAD

In 1926 at the Brown Derby Restaurant in Los Angeles, the owner, Bob Cobb, was trying to use up leftovers, rather than throw food out. He combined Roquefort cheese, avocado, celery, tomato, chives, watercress, hard-boiled eggs, chicken and bacon, and invented Cobb salad. What a crazy guy!

Ingredients:

> 10 lean pieces of bacon
> 4 hard-boiled eggs
> 1 whole romaine or cos lettuce, leaves separated
> and torn into bite-sized pieces
> Fresh herbs like rocket, cress, fennel, lemon balm,
> coriander and mint
> 2 handfuls watercress, chopped
> 2 cooked chicken breasts
> 2 avocados, pitted, peeled and diced
> 3 chopped tomatoes
> 125g crumbled Roquefort or Danish blue cheese
> 2 dessertspoons red wine vinegar
> 1 teaspoon Worcestershire sauce
> 1 teaspoon Dijon-style or grained mustard
> 1 garlic clove, peeled and crushed
> ¼ teaspoon rock salt
> ½ teaspoon coarsely ground black pepper
> 3 tablespoons extra virgin olive oil
> 10 chopped chives to garnish

Method:
1 Fry the bacon for 10 minutes until crisp. Cool them crumble.
2 Peel the hard-boiled eggs and cut into quarters.
3 In a large salad bowl, lay in the lettuce and place the egg quarters, bacon, herbs, watercress, chicken, avocados, tomatoes and all but a quarter of the blue cheese artistically on the lettuce.
4 In a bowl, blend together the wine vinegar, Worcester sauce, mustard, garlic, salt and pepper with a fork, and stir in the remaining cheese to form a paste. Slowly add the olive oil to complete the dressing.
5 Pour some of the dressing onto the salad, garnish with the chives and serve immediately. Serve the rest of the dressing separately. This makes four good-sized servings.

HE-MAN WINTER SALAD

This salad is ideal for winters when it is dark and cold, and the soldier inside you wants to feel alive and like marching into spring.

The tomato is botanically speaking, a fruit, but easier to think of it as a vegetable.

The beefsteak tomato was created by Johann Heinrich Muster in New York. He was awarded an American flag by the president of the United States for his achievement. That was nice.

Ingredients:

> 2 eggs, hard-boiled and cut into quarters
> 2 carrots, grated
> 1 tomato, roughly chopped
> 2 cooked beetroots, roughly diced
> A small bunch of parsley, finely chopped
> Half a bag of spinach (250g), washed
> 100g turnip (quarter of a small turnip), grated

Put them all into a bowl and stir in some He-Man vinaigrette dressing:

Ingredients:

> 3 tablespoons olive oil
> 1 tablespoon vinegar
> ½ teaspoon Dijon mustard
> Salt and pepper

Put the vinaigrette ingredients into a screw-top jar and shake them well until they thicken. A teaspoon of sherry will give it an extra kick.

You can add a cooked chicken breast, shredded, if you want more than a starter.

MUSTARD

Mustard is made from the seeds of mustard plants – the familiar yellow mustard, or it can be brown or black. It is all a bit confusing. Yellow mustard seeds are often referred to as white, and brown mustard seeds are sometimes called black. Whole, ground, cracked or pulverised mustard seeds are mixed with vinegar and water and other flavourings and made into a thick paste. Mustard often has a sharp, pungent flavour, and it is the mixing of the seed with cold liquid which causes the release of the enzyme myrosinase which provides the heat in mustard. Great for burgers, hot dogs and some cheeses – use it in salad dressings, soups and marinades.

All you need to do is mix equal parts mustard flour or powder and water to make a simple smooth prepared mustard. You can introduce other flavours, adding herbs, spices, salt or vinegars, or use the juice and zest of fruits to sweeten it. To make grainy mustards, soak the seeds in a liquid overnight before grinding or pulverising them in a blender. Soak dried fruit that you might want to add along with the seeds. Try a little turmeric for colouring.

Here are a couple of basic recipes to start you off – one using beer to soak the seed in, the other using wine.

THYME AND ALE MUSTARD

Ingredients:
>   5 tablespoons brown mustard seeds
>   5 tablespoons yellow mustard seeds
>   225ml real ale or stout
>   1 tablespoon mustard flour
>   1 tablespoon dried minced onion
>   2 teaspoons dried thyme leaves
>   150ml cider vinegar
>   1 teaspoon salt

Method:
1   Soak the mustard seeds in the ale overnight.
2   Stir the mustard flour, minced onion and thyme into the ale seed mixture and allow it to stand for 20 minutes.
3   Put the mustard mixture into a blender with the vinegar and salt.
4   Blend it until you get it to form a paste, with some seeds remaining visible.
5   Spoon into a glass jar with a tight lid and refrigerate before using.

SUN-DRIED TOMATO AND BASIL MUSTARD

Ingredients:
>   5 tablespoons brown mustard seeds
>   5 tablespoons yellow mustard seeds
>   10 sun-dried tomato halves
>   300ml dry white wine
>   4 teaspoons mustard flour
>   75ml of white wine vinegar
>   5 tablespoons fresh basil leaves, chopped
>   ½ teaspoon salt

Method:
1   Soak the mustard seeds and sun-dried tomatoes in the wine overnight.
2   Mix the soaked seeds with the other ingredients in your blender and blend to form a paste.
3   Spoon into a glass jar with a tight lid and refrigerate before using.

Pope John XXII, who was around in the early 1300s, was a great fan of mustard and to be sure of tasty supplies he created the post of Mustard-Maker to the Pope – who could certainly cut the mustard.

SPECIAL BUTTER

And while we are on the subject of mixing up mustards, let's not forget "special butter". It is the small touches which impress – why not spend a few minutes making your butter unforgettable?

EASY GARLIC BUTTER
125g softened butter
½ teaspoon garlic powder

EASY GARLIC AND CHIVE BUTTER
Add 2 teaspoons chopped chives to garlic butter.

EASY HERB BUTTER
Add 1 teaspoon chopped basil and ½ teaspoon dried oregano to the garlic and chive butter.

EASY PARSLEY AND GARLIC BUTTER
Add 1 tablespoon chopped parsley to the garlic butter.

GARLIC BREAD

Slice an ordinary baguette, not cutting quite all the way through, at an angle, every inch or so along. Butter each slice carefully and close the bread back up. Wrap it in foil and put it in an oven preheated to 180°C, gas mark 4, for about 20 minutes. If you want it browned on top, remove the foil and put it back in the oven for a few minutes. Serve to applause.

The tricky thing about garlic breath is that you can't really smell it yourself. So when you are having an intense conversation in the pub after dinner and your audience keels over, you need to do something fast. Chewing a few sprigs of parsley does help, but you can't really get rid of it. Chewing gum as a guest at dinner isn't really an option, nor is gargling with the Beaujolais.

But I can tell you that it is water and fat that reduce garlic breath, so milk or a latte or a real go at the vanilla ice cream is the best answer.

FOR STARTERS

FIRST COURSE CONFIDENCE!

Starters or appetizers are food items served before the main dish.

Any food served prior to the main course is technically an hors d'oeuvre.

A substantial starter or first course served at the table might be referred to as an entrée. A bit puzzling really. Why have an appetiser if you are hungry – why not get stuck in to the main dish straight away? Whatever you call it, it prolongs the whole dining experience and should be encouraged!

Soup! There are wonderful soups these days in cartons and tins which simply need reheated, but, once you have made your own and see how easy it is, you will never buy ready-made again. Soup is another opportunity to express yourself and exercise your imagination.

The word "soup" comes from a medieval word related to "sop" – a hunk of bread dunked in roast drippings. The earliest evidence of soup being made goes back to around 6000 BC, with archaeologists identifying that it was made from hippopotamus bones!

WHAT IS STOCK?

Stock is the liquid which is left over after food such as chicken, other meat, vegetables or bones have been boiled in water. It is a great base for soups, stews and sauces, and can be kept for a few days in the fridge, or frozen and kept for longer. Often recipes will state that stock is needed. There are excellent stock cubes readily available, with clear instructions on how to make up the stock. You can also use a spoonful of meat extract dissolved in boiling water if you haven't got any cubes.

MAKING STOCK

Making stock is easy, and apart from making soup with it, you can add great flavour to foods by simply substituting stock for all or part of the water specified in a recipe. Try it next time you are making boiled rice.

The main types of stock are based on chicken, meat, vegetables and fish.

CHICKEN STOCK

Chicken stock is easily made using the bones and the rest of the carcass after you have cooked a whole chicken.

Ingredients:
    Whole chicken carcass
    1 onion, roughly chopped
    2 carrots, roughly chopped
    2 or 3 sticks of celery, roughly chopped
    4 garlic cloves, peeled and chopped
    1 tablespoon whole black peppercorns
    Any other leftover vegetables

Method:
1   Put the ingredients into a large saucepan, cover with water, bring to the boil and simmer for about 2 hours.
2   Skim off the foam which rises to the surface from time to time with a large spoon. The volume of liquid will reduce as it simmers.

3   When the time is up, strain the stock through a sieve, allow it to cool, and refrigerate it in a jug or bowl for a few hours.
4   The fat will settle at the top of the stock and can be easily spooned off. The stock is now ready to use or freeze.

VEGETABLE STOCK

You can use just about all kinds of vegetables for this stock (but best not to use sprouts, broccoli or cauliflower) – and go easy on tomatoes as these too will dominate the flavour.

Yes to onions, potatoes, sweet potatoes, carrots, celery, peas, sweetcorn, parsley, green beans, peppers, mushrooms, garlic, shallots, fresh basil and other herbs. Cover your ingredients with water, bring to the boil and simmer for about an hour. Cool and strain the stock and discard the residue. The stock is now ready to use or freeze.

MEAT STOCK

Simmer leftover meat and bones with vegetables.

Ingredients:
>   Meat bones and leftover meat
>   2 onions, roughly chopped
>   4 carrots, roughly chopped
>   4 sticks of celery, roughly chopped
>   6 cloves of garlic, peeled and chopped
>   2 chopped tomatoes
>   2 bay leaves
>   1 tablespoon whole black peppercorns
>   A few sprigs of parsley, basil and thyme

Method:
1   Put the ingredients into a large saucepan, cover with water, bring to the boil and simmer for about 3 hours. Keep the pan covered with a lid to prevent the liquid reducing too much.
2   Skim off the foam which rises to the surface from time to time with a large spoon.

3   When the time is up, strain the stock through a sieve, let it cool, and refrigerate it in a jug or bowl for a few hours.
4   The fat will settle at the top of the stock and can be easily spooned off. The stock is now ready to use or freeze.

FISH STOCK

The same idea – you can use fish scraps, bones, shells, trimmings and leftovers.

Ingredients:
>   Fish scraps
>   2 tablespoons butter
>   2 onions, chopped
>   4 garlic cloves, peeled and chopped
>   1 stick of celery, finely chopped
>   Juice of a small lemon or lime
>   1 tablespoon parsley, chopped
>   1 teaspoon whole black peppercorns
>   A splash or two of leftover dry white wine,
>   if you have it

Ingredients:
1   Melt the butter in the saucepan and gently fry the onion, garlic and celery until the onion becomes transparent.
2   Add the rest of the ingredients, cover with water, bring to the boil then simmer for about an hour. Keep the pan covered with a lid to prevent the liquid reducing too much.
3   Cool and strain the stock and discard the residue. The stock is now ready to use or freeze.

GRUEL

The simplest kind of soup – it will soon come back into fashion in these austere times. You need cereal – such as oats, wheat or rye flour, or rice. Boil it in water or, to make it slightly luxurious, milk. The aim is to make a thin, runny porridge. Garnish with chopped dandelion greens from the park, and croutons made of old stale bread. Peasant chic for your next dinner party.

FRENCH ONION SOUP

French Onion Soup was invented by King Louis XV. Taking a break at his hunting lodge, all he could rustle up for tea was a couple of onions, some cheese and champagne. Clever chap stewed it.

Can't have been much of a hunter though.

Ingredients:

> 500g onions, thinly sliced
> 1 litre beef stock
> 25g butter
> Salt and pepper

Method:

1 Cook the onion slowly in the butter until soft and golden – it will take about 20 minutes.

2 Add the stock, bring to the boil, cover and simmer for 20 minutes.

3 Check for seasoning and serve with toasted slices of baguette on top.

To make this the way the French Foreign Legion like it best, lightly butter the slices of baguette and sprinkle them with grated cheese. Ladle the soup into ovenproof bowls, put a slice or two of the bread on top, and put into a moderate oven (180°C, gas mark 4) for about 10 minutes, or under a moderate grill for 5 minutes, or until the cheese has melted and browned slightly.

GREEN PEA SOUP

Mint is a nice addition to pea soup. Add a few sprigs when adding the peas.

Ingredients:
>500g fresh or frozen green peas (weigh fresh peas after shelling)
>1 litre stock
>1 small onion, chopped
>Knob of butter
>1 lettuce, leaves separated, washed and shredded
>Salt and pepper
>2 tablespoons double cream

Method:
1   If you are using fresh peas, shell the peas, and wash and keep half the pods. If you are not using pods skip to step 4.
2   In a large saucepan, bring the stock to the boil. Add pods and seasoning, then simmer for 30 minutes.
3   Take the pan off the heat. If you have a blender or liquidiser, liquidise once it is cool enough. Then strain this mixture through a sieve and discard the solids and keep the stock.
4   In a pot, melt a little butter and fry the onion till soft.
5   Now put the stock into this pot, add the lettuce and peas, (and mint if you are using it) and simmer until peas are tender, about 10 minutes or so. Liquidise the soup or pass it through a sieve, and put it back into the saucepan.
6   Check for seasoning. Stir in the cream, and serve.

CREAM OF SWEETCORN SOUP

Ingredients:
>200g sweetcorn (fresh, frozen or canned)
>1 stick of celery, chopped
>A small piece of turnip, chopped
>1 small onion, chopped
>1 bay leaf
>1 litre stock
>25g plain flour
>25g butter
>250ml milk
>2 tablespoons cream
>2 egg yolks
>Salt and pepper

Method:
1   Put all the vegetables, the bay leaf and the stock into a large pan and bring to the boil. Simmer for 30–45 minutes until all the vegetables are tender.
2   With the flour, butter and milk, make a white sauce (see page 49), and stir it into the soup.
3   If you have a blender or liquidiser, liquidise the soup once it is cool enough. Otherwise pass it through a sieve into a large bowl, rubbing the mixture through the sieve using a wooden spoon. Put it back into the pan, check it for seasoning, and bring it to the boil.
4   Mix the egg yolks and cream in a bowl. Pour some hot (not boiling) soup into this, stirring it well. Then stir the egg mixture into the soup, and heat it through gently, but be careful not to let it boil.

If you are too tight to buy your good lady flowers, why not serve up garnishes of sweetcorn "daisies" with the end bits of your corn on the cob. Romantic!

TORTELLINI IN BRODO

One of the best standbys to have in the cupboard is a tin or two of beef or chicken consommé. Consommé is a clear soup.

1. Mix the consommé half and half with water (one tin will serve two people), put it into a saucepan, and heat it gently.
2. Add some fresh tortellini (or dried pasta) and follow the instructions – usually you will need to simmer them for 4 minutes (longer for dried pasta). As the soup simmers, sprinkle in some herbs and black pepper.

MEATBALL SOUP

Here is another great standby using beef consommé.

There are some great frozen meatballs to be had from these small express supermarkets, or even from all-night garages that sell food.

1. Tip the meatballs out of their bag onto a baking tray, or a flat cake tin, and heat in the oven – usually for about 15 minutes – it tells you on the bag.
2. When the meatballs have been in for 10 minutes, put the consommé in a saucepan to heat gently, mixed half and half with water (one tin will serve two people). Add some frozen peas or sweetcorn and simmer for 4 minutes. As the soup simmers, sprinkle in some herbs and black pepper.
3. Remove the meatballs from the oven, add to the soup, and serve.

CORN ON THE COB

Corn on the cob was sold on the streets of New York City in the early 19th century by barefoot "hot corn girls" – a bit like the hot dog and bagel stands that you see today.

Ingredients:

> 4 cobs of fresh corn, trimmed
> Salt, chopped parsley and butter (to serve)

Method:

1 Fill a large pot three-quarters full with cold water and bring to the boil.
2 Add the corn cobs, bring back to the boil, and boil for 5 minutes.
3 Remove the cobs from the water and serve immediately with butter, salt and parsley.

The art of eating corn on the cob is something to be practical about. It is possible to utilise two forks jabbed into each end as handles, but you can buy screw-in holders, which are perhaps more delicate. This is a bib napkin experience, as the butter will drip as you chomp your way around the cob, hoovering all the bits off. This is caveman style, so perhaps not the ideal starter for a first date. Floss or toothpicks essential.

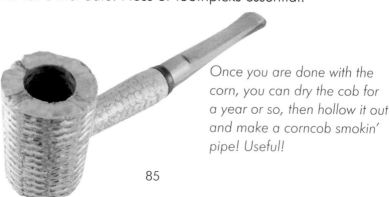

Once you are done with the corn, you can dry the cob for a year or so, then hollow it out and make a corncob smokin' pipe! Useful!

PÂTÉ

Yet another excuse to be creative. You can put just about anything in pâté.

You can make pâté with chicken livers, duck livers, mushrooms, crab, salmon or olives, to mention a few. And once you have tasted it, give it a fancy name. Pâté de foie gras is the ultimate form of this delicacy. Foie gras is French for "fat liver" and it is made from the livers of fattened geese or ducks.

Ingredients:
250g chicken livers, cleaned and chopped
2 tablespoons butter
75g softened cream cheese
2 tablespoons brandy
1 teaspoon salt
¼ teaspoon pepper
½ teaspoon dried thyme
¼ teaspoon nutmeg

Method:
1   In a heavy frying pan, brown the livers in the butter over a medium heat for about 6–8 minutes, moving them around with a spatula as they fry.
2   Put the livers into an electric blender with all the residue from the pan, together with the other ingredients. Blend for 30 seconds or until the mixture is smooth.
3   Taste and add more seasoning if required.
4   Spoon the mixture into a bowl, cover, and chill in the fridge for 8 hours.
5   Additions to the basic ingredients will offer variety, colour and texture – perhaps some slivers of red or green peppers, mushrooms etc.
6   Serve tastefully and delicately with sliced baguette.

PRAWN COCKTAIL

Serge asked, "What's the difference between a shrimp and a prawn?" Many people refer to a shrimp as a prawn, but a shrimp is a shrimp; a prawn is a prawn not a shrimp. The difference is size. Some places say small and medium shrimp are sold simply as shrimp, and large, king, and jumbo shrimp are called prawns. Elsewhere all shrimp, regardless of size, are sold as shrimp, and in some markets they are prawns. So what about the shrimp's relative, the Dublin Bay prawn, which in Italy is called scampi? In the USA scampi is often the name on the menu for shrimp but is the culinary name for some kinds of lobster.

So that's cleared that up! Let's make a prawn cocktail.

Ingredients:
4 tablespoons thick mayonnaise
4 tablespoons cream
4 teaspoons tomato ketchup
300g fresh prawns (cooked, peeled and chilled)
or use frozen cooked prawns (300g defrosted weight)
1 small lettuce, washed and torn into strips
Cayenne pepper or paprika
Chopped parsley or slices of hard-boiled egg to garnish
4 slices of lemon

Method:
1   Mix the mayonnaise with the cream and the tomato ketchup.
2   Wash and dry the prawns and fold them into the mayonnaise mixture.
3   Line four small bowls or wide cocktail glasses with the lettuce strips.
4   Spoon the mayonnaise and prawn mixture into the two serving bowls, and sprinkle with cayenne pepper or paprika.
5   Garnish with a little parsley, or a small slice of hard-boiled egg.
6   Serve with a slice of lemon at the edge of the bowl or cut and placed on the glass.

PRAWNS IN AVOCADO

Avocado is a great vehicle, halved, like a boat, for a starter. An avocado ready to eat should be soft but not squashy. If it is too hard, leave it for a day or two until it has ripened. When inspecting avocados in the supermarket, be discreet – do not press too hard and burst the skin. If you do, put it back and pretend it wasn't you.

Method:
1   Cut the avocado in half and remove the stone.
2   Prepare as you would for a prawn cocktail, placing an elegant sufficiency in the centre of the halved avocado, filling the hollow where the stone has been plus a bit more. (An elegant sufficiency is a heaped tablespoon.)

BREAD

The perfect way to serve soup or pâté or a prawn starter is to accompany it with some fresh home-made bread – the whole loaf on the table, with some slices ready cut, but still on the bread board. Start by making a white loaf – then after a few attempts, introduce different flours of your choice. Brown or wholemeal bread goes better with most starters. Serve with butter.

WHITE BREAD

Ingredients:
> 500g strong white bread flour
> 2 level teaspoons salt
> 25g lard
> 15g fresh yeast or 7g dried yeast
> 1 level teaspoon sugar
> 250ml lukewarm water

Method:
1. Warm a large mixing bowl. Add the salt to the flour and mix it in, and rub in the lard (see pages 31, 179 for rubbing in).
2. If you are using fresh yeast, dissolve the sugar in half the warm water, sprinkle in the yeast and leave to froth. If you are using dried yeast, refer to the instructions on the sachet.
3. Add the yeast liquid or dried yeast to the flour along with the remaining liquid, to make an elastic dough. It should be soft but not sticky.
4. Sprinkle some flour on

your work surface and turn the dough out onto it. Knead the dough well for 10 minutes. Yes, it's hard work but Legionnaires are strong men and are used to it.

5   Put the dough back into the bowl and cover it with clingfilm or a plastic bag brushed with a little oil to stop it sticking. Or put it in a large lightly oiled plastic bag. Place it in a warm place to rise for 1 hour, or until it doubles in size.

5   Turn it out and knead it again for a few minutes.

6   Shape the dough into a loaf, and place it in a large warm greased bread tin, making sure it is just three-quarters full.

7   Cover the loaf with a lightly oiled plastic bag or clingfilm again, and leave it to rise until the dough is at the top of the tin.

8   Put it into a very hot oven, 230°C, gas mark 8, then reduce the heat to 190°C, gas mark 5, and bake for 1 hour.

9   Remove the bread from the tin by turning it onto a wire cooling rack, tapping the tin gently to release it. The loaf should sound hollow when given a sharp tap.

Now that you have the basic recipe, you can experiment with different flours – perhaps half and half white and brown or wholemeal flour. Or working within the basic flour weight, substitute a little oatmeal or a handful of porridge oats. You will get an eye for your dough – whether it needs a little more water, or if it seems too wet – add a little more flour.

PIZZA

Naples is a city rich in gastronomy. Neapolitan cuisine has brought the world Neapolitan ice cream (chocolate, vanilla and strawberry, side by side) and PIZZA!

To make 3 pizzas:
> 350g strong white flour
> 6g dried yeast
> 1 teaspoon salt
> 1 tablespoon olive oil
> 240ml lukewarm water

Method:
1 Sift the flour, salt and yeast into a mixing bowl, and stir in the water and olive oil to make a soft dough, as in the bread recipe (page 91).
2 Knead the dough by hand, on a well-floured worktop, for 10 minutes.
3 Put the dough back into the bowl and cover it, or put it into an oiled plastic bag, as in the bread recipe. Leave it to rise in a warm place for an hour or until doubled in size.
4 Take the pizza dough out of the bowl and knead it for a minute or two.
5 Divide the dough into 3 equal portions and roll them into balls.
6 Using a rolling pin, roll them out flat so that they are about 1cm thick. Or you can pull them out flat using your hands. Pinch the edges to make a rim.
7 Place the rounds of dough on an oiled baking tray or trays. Your pizza bases are now ready for their toppings.

PIZZA TOPPINGS

Ingredients:
Tomato purée
Mozzarella cheese
Grated hard cheese (such as cheddar)
Tomatoes
Olives, ham, slices of pepperoni and/or peppers

Method:
1   Spread some tomato purée on the pizza base.
2   Slice the mozzarella cheese thinly and place the slices on top.
3   Add the other ingredients as you like.
4   Bake in a hot oven (220°C, gas mark 7) for about 20 minutes.

Be creative. The pizza base is a vehicle. Smoked salmon? Why not?

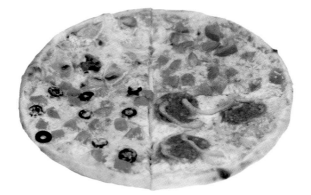

HOW TO COOK FISH

A cod supper is not so common now at the chippie. The fish more likely to be battered is Alaskan pollock or Vietnamese catfish, or pangasius – usually known by the name river cobbler. People are looking for lower-priced items than cod and haddock. Mussels and warm water prawns and scallops are becoming more popular. Plaice is very expensive and coley is difficult to get. The river cobbler is a mild-tasting white fish and is a great substitute for cod and haddock. Pollock tends to be used for fish fingers or breaded fish bites.

Fish is good for you – wild marine fish contains omega-3 fatty acids, which are good for the brain and the heart – and that's not a load of cobblers!

You will remember from what I told you already that all fish contains protein. It has a certain amount of fat too. In some fish the fat is stored in the liver and these are called white fish. You will have heard of cod liver oil and halibut liver oil, which are extracted from the liver of the fish and used as medicinal food. In other kinds of fish the fat is distributed throughout the body of the fish and these are called oily fish. Vitamins A and D are also found in oily fish. Herring, mackerel and salmon are examples of oily fish. Skate, sole and plaice are white fish. Look in the fishmonger's shop or fresh fish counter of the supermarket and see what other fish are on sale. Ask the fishmonger for advice – fishmongers are happy to help.

Fish does not keep very well so it is best to cook it the day it is bought. There are several points to look for when buying fish. It should feel firm and not flabby and be bright in colour. Fish with scales should be bright and silvery and there should be plenty of scales. When the fish gets stale, the scales dry up and fall off. The eyes should be full and bright red. Plaice has spots on the dark side and these must be a good reddish colour. Shellfish should be heavy in proportion to its size. Fish naturally smells "fishy" but it should not have an unpleasant smell. When stale, the strong smell might remind you of ammonia.

Small whole fish like whiting or slices of fish like cod and hake may be poached. We often speak of "boiled" fish, but this is not correct because the fish should not be boiled or it will break up and be tasteless. The right term is to "poach". Only a little water is used and the cooking must be done gently.

TO POACH FISH

Put enough cold water into a pan just to cover the fish. Add half a level teaspoon salt, 1 teaspoon lemon juice or vinegar and 2–3 peppercorns to each 300ml water. Put in the fish, bring just to boiling point, then lower the heat and simmer very gently. For thin fillets of fish allow 3 minutes, for thicker fillets, 5 minutes, and for cutlets of fish or thick slices allow 7–10 minutes. Remove the fish with a fish slice and, as it may look a little dull, serve with a sprig of parsley or a wedge of lemon.

Refer to the recipe for white sauce (page 49) and decide what sauce you will serve with your fish. To make a good meal, serve mashed potatoes and peas or carrots with the fish.

TO FRY FISH

Frying is a popular way of cooking fish. It is suitable for small whole plaice or sole, or fillets or cutlets of cod, hake, halibut, etc. To improve the appearance of the fish and to make it easier to remove from the pan, it is coated before frying with flour, or egg and breadcrumbs, or batter. Flour is the simplest coating, so try starting with this recipe.

TO FRY A CUTLET OF COD

Many people like chips with fried fish. Tomatoes and peas are good too, as they add colour. You could also try to garnish it with a little salad.

1   Wash the fish and pat it dry on a piece of kitchen paper.
2   Put 2 level tablespoons of flour on a plate, add a pinch of salt and a shake of pepper and mix with the flour.
3   Press the fish into the flour, turn it over and coat the other side.
4   Heat about 60g of oil in a frying pan. The exact amount depends on the size of the pan, but the fat should be a good 6mm deep in the pan. The heat of the oil is very important, and as you are learning to cook you really should test it because, unless you are very experienced, it is difficult to know when it is hot enough.

4   You can test it this way. Cut a small cube of bread, and when you think the fat should be hot enough, put in the bread, which should brown in just under 1 minute. If it browns almost immediately, the oil is too hot and you must draw it away from the heat and leave it to cool down. If the bread shows no sign of browning in 1 minute, heat it a little longer and try again. When you are satisfied that the oil is about right, put the fish in gently. Try not to splash.

5   Cook for 4 minutes, then, using a fish slice in one hand and a palette knife in the other, turn the fish over. Now turn down the heat a little and cook for another 5–6 minutes according to the thickness of the cutlet.

6   While the fish is cooking, put a piece of kitchen paper on to a plate ready for draining. Lift the fish from the pan and put it on the paper to drain off any surplus oil. Then put it on to a hot plate or serving dish with a sprig of parsley and a wedge of lemon.

7   If you are frying thin fillets of plaice or sole allow about 5 minutes altogether; thicker fillets of cod or haddock will take 7–10 minutes.

TO BAKE WHITE FISH

The fish should be prepared as before and put into a greased ovenproof dish. Sprinkle it with salt and pepper and a squeeze of lemon juice and dot with butter.

Cover with the lid of the dish or with greased foil or greased paper and bake in a fairly hot oven, 190°C, gas mark 5.

Allow 15–25 minutes, according to the thickness of the fish.

Tomatoes can be baked in the oven at the same time.

Remember to put a little parsley and lemon on the serving dish. [Steaming is also a good method of cooking white fish (see page 101). Fillets of plaice, sole or whiting are most suitable.]

TO GRILL FISH

1   Wash and pat the fish dry – it is not necessary to coat it with flour or batter. When the grill is hot, brush the bars of the grid in the grill pan with a little melted oil.
2   Place the fish on the grid, brush it with more oil and sprinkle lightly with salt and pepper. Put it under the hot grill and leave for about 5 minutes until the surface is nicely browned.
3   Use a fish slice and palette knife as when frying a cutlet of cod (page 98), and turn the fish over. Brush this side with oil, add seasoning again and put it back under the grill.
4   Cook a further 5 minutes and it should be done. You should now be able to decide for yourself what to serve with it to make a good meal.

TO GRILL A SOLE

Think of the appearance of the dish as well as the food value. If you are grilling thin fillets of sole or plaice, it will not be necessary to turn the fish while it is cooking.

Sole is a flatfish. The name sole comes from its resemblance to a sandal or the sole of a shoe (Latin – solea). In Germany and Spain they think it looks more like a tongue. I prefer the shoe.

100

TO STEAM FILLETS OF FISH

Wash the fillets, pat them dry and place them on an ovenproof plate that will fit over the top of a saucepan. Grease the plate with butter and put the fish on to it. Large fillets can be folded over. Sprinkle the fish with salt and pepper, add a knob of butter and 1 tablespoon of milk.

Cover with another plate or put a piece of buttered paper on top and cover with the lid of the saucepan.

Half fill the saucepan with water and stand the plate on top. When the water boils, lower the heat and let the water simmer. The fillets will take about 10 minutes to cook.

Serve with a sprig of parsley and a slice of lemon.

TO COOK OILY FISH

All the methods described so far have been for white fish. Oily fish needs slightly different treatment. Kippers are the only oily fish suitable for poaching. This can be done in a dish deep enough to cover the fish with water.

Put the fish into the dish, pour on boiling water, cover tightly and leave for 5 minutes. Pour off the water and serve the kippers with a small knob of butter. This method gives a lightly cooked kipper, which many people enjoy, but you could pop it under the grill for a minute or so before serving if you prefer.

Herrings, mackerel and sprats can be fried. It is not necessary to coat them and they can be fried without oil or just with the minimum of oil.

Smoked fish like kippers and bloaters do need a little oil, as some of their natural oil is lost in the smoking process.

TICKLED TROUT WITH ALMONDS

Trout tickling is the ancient poacher's art of tickling the underside of a trout with your fingers, which puts the trout into a trance, allowing the tickler to scoop it out of the water and hurl it onto the bank. No nets, rods or lines required! Better, more fun and fairer to cast a fly, catch it then tickle it when you get home!

Trout was traditionally eaten coated in oats, as this was something affordable and very easily obtained. Cooking trout with almonds would have been considered a much more exotic method.

You will need (for two people):
>1 fly rod, waders and a packed lunch
>2 trout, each 250g, gutted
>2 tablespoons plain flour, seasoned with salt and pepper
>1 tablespoon cooking oil
>50g butter
>50g flaked almonds
>Juice of a small lemon

Method:
1   Wash the trout under cold running water and then dry them (kitchen paper towels are great for this), then roll them in the seasoned flour.
2   Heat half the butter and the oil in a frying pan over a medium heat and fry the fish for about 5–7 minutes on each side.
3   Remove them from the pan and keep them warm.
4   Wipe the pan clean with kitchen paper, put in some more butter and melt it over a moderate heat. Add the almonds and fry them gently for a minute or two until they are brown.
5   Place the hot trout on warmed plates or a serving dish, squeezing lemon juice over each fish.
6   Spoon the almonds over the fish. Serve with potatoes of your choice and green beans.

NICE OLD TROUT

I've recently been observing Serge's social networking antics with great amusement. None more so than his use of foodie messageboards as a means of meeting women: "WLTM MILF with GSOH and own food processor". He's had great success; if by success you mean that I have had a bloody good laugh and been able to come off my anti-depressants for a whole week. The nice lady above has just received Serge's beach wear photos. What a treat!

SHELLFISH

Shellfish are marine animals with shells, and the name can refer to anything from clams and oysters to lobster and shrimp, as well as octopus and squid. They have been enjoyed all over the world for thousands of years.

Be careful when cooking for guests! Shellfish allergy is one of the most common food allergies. Some people have an allergy only to certain kinds of shellfish, while others are allergic to all.

Seafood splits into two classifications, fish and shellfish. In turn, you can divide shellfish into two sub-groups: molluscs and crustaceans. Crustaceans include crab, crayfish, lobster and shrimp. Molluscs have three further sub-groups:
    Bivalve: clams, mussels, oysters, scallops
    Univalve: abalone, conch, snails
    Cephalopod: octopus, squid.

Some folk classify fish and shellfish by environment – whether they are freshwater or saltwater dwellers; or surface or bottom feeders; or temperate or tropical. Then you have anadromous fish, which migrate from the sea to fresh waters (such as salmon), and then catadromous that go the other way (such as eels) which head out to sea from fresh water to spawn.

Fascinating!

MOULES MARINIÈRE

À la marinière is French for 'mariner's style'. The French Navy, officially the Marine Nationale, and particularly les Fusiliers Marins, and the Commandos de Marine love their moules. If there are no friendly navy divers around, you will need 2kg of fresh mussels from a quality fishmonger or quayside stall – but you must buy them on the day that you are going to cook them. There is a bit of preparation needed, as you have to scrape and scrub each mussel to remove any barnacles and pull off the beard. This is best done by putting the mussels in a basin and scraping them under cold running water. Discard any mussels that are not completely closed.

Mussels only need steamed in a small amount of liquid. When they open in cooking, they release liquid which is quite salty, so don't add much extra salt.

Ingredients:
>   2 tablespoons olive oil
>   3 garlic cloves, peeled and crushed
>   2 small shallots, or a small onion, finely chopped
>   300ml white wine
>   A pinch of salt
>   Black pepper
>   A few sprigs fresh thyme
>   4 large fresh basil leaves
>   2kg mussels
>   300ml water
>   25g butter
>   Chopped fresh parsley, to garnish

Method:
1   Fry the garlic and shallots in oil for 2–3 minutes.
2   Add the wine, salt and pepper, herbs and mussels. Bring to the boil and cover the pan tightly. Simmer for 5 minutes. Hold the lid tight and shake the pan gently every minute or so.
3   With a slotted spoon, take out the mussels, place them on a warmed serving dish and keep hot.
4   Add the water and butter to the pan and bring back to a fast boil for 4 minutes, reducing the liquid.
5   Pour the liquid over the mussels and garnish with parsley. Serve with home-made bread or baguette.

Any mussels which do not
open during cooking should
be thrown away as they could
be dangerous to eat.

PRAWNS POACHED IN WINE AND CREAM

Don't choose a cheap wine for this recipe just because it's for cooking with. It needn't be the best there is, but at least choose one that you would be happy drinking on its own, so have a glass while you work!

Ingredients:
>450g freshly peeled Scottish prawns
>25g butter
>1 onion, chopped
>300ml white wine
>1 clove of garlic, chopped or crushed
>50ml double cream
>1 tablespoon dry pale sherry
>Salt and pepper
>Chopped parsley and chopped dill

Method:
1 Wash the prawns and dry them on kitchen paper.
2 Melt the butter in a shallow pan and fry the onion gently for around 5 minutes until it is just soft.
3 Pour in the white wine, add the chopped or crushed garlic, and bring to a slow simmer.
4 Add the prawns and the cream and poach with the lid on the pan for around 10–15 minutes. Taste the sauce and season. If you like, add one tablespoon of dry sherry
5 Add a generous handful of chopped parsley and a little chopped dill, and serve with bread or floury boiled potatoes. Serves 2.

THE LOBSTER

Lobsters are worthy opponents – we have respect for these marine crustaceans. They have a hard protective shell, antennae and five sets of pincers and have inspired many frontline combat armoured tank designers. Not the best dish to choose if you are very hungry, but certainly an impressive selection!

Most lobsters are dark green and black or brown in colour. They only turn bright red once they are properly cooked.

Choosing a lobster is interesting. It is probably watching you. You are looking for as active a lobster as possible with a tail that should curl under when it is lifted. Best to have a shopping bag if you are travelling from the shops by bus, and if some annoying child is staring at you from the seat in front, simply bring out your lobster and inspect it.

Lobster should be cooked in salty water with some wine and herbs (parsley, and a bay leaf if you have one to hand) and a few vegetables – I think celery and carrots with a small onion chopped and tossed in, which all combines to make a delicious stock or sauce. It isn't an exact science – but don't overdo the salt.

A dry white wine is best – but the lobster won't be too fussy.

One of the world's great debates is about the most humane way to cook a lobster. Being boiled alive doesn't appeal to me! One recommended way is to put the lobster in a dish in the freezer for 10 minutes or until it is unconscious, before boiling. Or, quicker, slice a sharp knife quickly through its head, right between or just below the eyes. (You could ask your fishmonger to do this for you.) You can steam or grill lobster too – but I like a good boiling and the stock that is produced.

BOILED LOBSTER

Ingredients:
>1 lobster
>Sea salt
>A glass of dry white wine
>1 onion, chopped
>1 carrot, chopped
>1 stick of celery, chopped
>A handful of chopped parsley
>1 bay leaf

Method:
1   Weigh the lobster, as you need to calculate how long to cook it for.
2   Put it in a dish in the freezer, and warn anyone else who might open the door to beware. Or quickly slice through its head.
3   You will obviously need a pot large enough to put your lobster in – and you need a lid for it. You need enough water so that the lobster will be completely immersed.
4   Add 1 tablespoon of sea salt for every 1 to 1½ litres of water.
5   Pour 2 glasses of dry white wine, add one, drink one.
6   Add the chopped onion, carrot, celery and parsley and the bay leaf.
7   Bring the soup to the boil and simmer for 5 minutes to get the best out of the vegetables, then bring back to a fierce boil.
8   Retrieve the lobster from the freezer, keeping away from the claws, and place it into the boiling water.
9   Cover with the lid, and when the soup comes back to the boil, boil the lobster for 10–12 minutes for the first 500g of weight and then 3 more minutes for each additional 500g. A 1kg lobster will take 15 minutes.
10 Take it out of the pot carefully to save the soup, then drain and serve.

HOW TO EAT LOBSTER

1   Twist off the legs – tasty meat inside!
2   Twist off the claws.
3   Remove the loose part of the claw.
4   Use a nutcracker to break the end off the large section of claw to expose the meat.
5   With a spoon handle, push the meat out.
6   Twist the tail and the lobster's back apart – the top of the tail has the lobster's digestive tract under it which should be removed before taking the rest of the tail meat.

The Antennae, antennules and the mouth parts are inedible, and avoid the green substance which is the lobster's digestive system.

COOKING MEAT

I was giving a lecture to the local DWROS group (older men – Divorcees, Widowers, Retirees and Old Soldiers), about food hygiene as part of a kind of corporate Assault Course which has become very popular since the local library closed.

I asked: "Have you any idea how dangerous food is?"

"What we stuff into our stomachs should have killed us years ago. Any meat badly cooked can be lethal. Undercooked poultry, vegetables coated in pesticides, and just think about the lead pipes and germs and chemicals in our drinking water. But there is one thing that is the most terrifying of all – and all of us eat it – and it's far more dangerous even than you old soldiers sticking your head above the trench! Can anyone here tell me what that lethal product I'm talking about is? ... Yes – you, sir. The fellow with the red tie."

The man bowed his head and said: "wedding cake."

HOW TO CHOOSE MEAT

We had a mess assistant in the Legion from Thailand who thought all meat was beef. Or maybe it was just a misunderstanding: "Do you want chicken beef or pork beef or normal beef?"

Meat is one of the main sources of protein. Beef is one of the best sources of protein, Vitamin B_{12}, niacin, zinc, Vitamin B_2 and iron.

If you look in a butcher's shop you might feel bewildered by all the different cuts of meat, but if you study the diagrams you will soon be able to recognise them. Butchers in different parts of the country cut their meat into slightly different joints, but the diagrams give you the general idea.

The internal organs are called offal. I have already told you about my love for this (see page 19) – liver, kidney, heart, tripe and sweetbreads.

Meat can be roasted, braised, boiled, stewed (either in a stew pan or in a casserole in the oven), fried or grilled. It is important to choose the right kind of meat for each particular method of cooking. It would be wasteful to stew a roasting joint, and if you try to roast or fry stewing meat it will never be tender.

WHAT TO LOOK FOR

See that beef is a good red colour and that it is interspersed with fat – so it should have a "marbled" appearance. The fat should be a pale yellow colour. Lamb is lighter in colour than beef and the fat should be hard and white. Pork has pale pink flesh and the fat is white but softer than that of lamb.

Whatever type of meat you buy, go for the very best quality you can find. It's better to have a smaller quantity of good meat than a large cut of a meat that has been factory farmed and processed.

Cuts and joints of beef:
1   Neck or sticking: stew or make soup or stock
2   Chuck or blade: stew or make soup or stock
3   Middle rib: roast
4   Top rib: roast
5   Fore rib: roast
6   Sirloin: roast or boned and rolled and roast
7   Rump: fry or grill
8   Aitchbone (or rump bone): roast
9   Topside and silverside: boil or salt and boil
10 and 11 Flank: stew or braise
12 and 13 Brisket: stew or braise
14   Shoulder: stew or make soups and stock
15   Shin: stew or make soup, stock or gravy beef
16   Leg: stew or make soup, stock or gravy beef

Cuts and joints of lamb and mutton:
1   Loin chump: roast
2   Leg: roast or boil
3   Loin: roast or cut into chops and fry
4   Best end neck: divide into cutlets and grill or roast
5   Middle neck: stew or braise
6   Scrag: stew or braise
7   Shoulder: roast

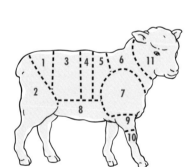

8 Breast: bone, stuff and roast or stew
9 Shank: stew
10 Trotter: stew
11 Head: make broth or stew

Cuts and joints of pork:
1 Head: bone, stuff and boil or use for brawn
2 Spare rib: roast
3 Hand and spring: roast
4 Loin: roast or cut into chops and fry
5 Belly: boil or stew, generally pickled
6 Leg: roast
7 Trotters: stew or use for stock

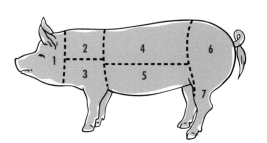

Cuts and joints of camel:
1 Neck or sticking: stew or make soup or stock
2 Chuck or blade: stew or make soup or stock
3 Middle rib: roast
4 Top rib: roast
5 Fore rib: roast
6 Sirloin: roast or boned and rolled and roast
7 Rump: fry or grill
8 Aitchbone (or rump bone): roast
9 Topside and silverside: boil or salt and boil
10 and 11 Flank: stew or braise
12 and 13 Brisket: stew or braise
14 Shoulder: stew or make soups and stock
15 Shin: stew or make soup, stock or gravy beef
16 Leg: stew or make soup, stock or gravy beef
17 (and possibly 18) Hump: roast in the same way as sirloin of beef. Use young camel meat only.

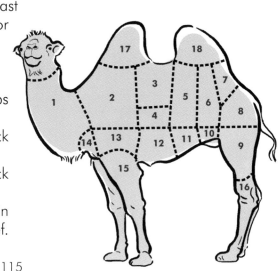

TIMES FOR ROASTING

In supermarkets and in many butcher's shops too, joints of meat are clearly marked with the weight and price per kilo and pound, but if your butcher cuts a joint for you be sure to ask how much it weighs. You need to know this when calculating the time for cooking. Generally allow so many minutes per pound or 450g, and then add a little extra. The time given in the chart below is for meat started in a preheated oven. Some people like to cook meat more slowly and for a longer time. You must allow a little longer if you use a double roaster or cook the meat in foil.

Meat	Minutes per 450g	Minutes longer
Beef	15–20	15–20
Lamb	20	20
Pork	25	25

CAMEL

The biggest item on any menu anywhere in the world is roast camel. Prepared like a "Russian doll", it is sometimes served at a Bedouin wedding celebration. The camel is stuffed with a sheep's carcass, which in turn has been stuffed with chickens, which have been stuffed with fish, which are stuffed with eggs and tomatoes.

MINCE

Mince is of course my signature dish. I have a special pot which I keep only for mince.

You can find this recipe along with another 71 essential life-sustaining mince recipes in my critically acclaimed work, *The Complete Book of Mince*. It is not so much a recipe to be made and eaten – it is more of a ceremony.

Ingredients:
> 500g lean steak mince
> 2 onions, chopped
> 2 carrots, sliced into circles
> 25g plain flour
> Approximately 250ml beef stock or gravy
> (Some people use gravy powder. If using gravy
> powder, omit the flour.)

Method:
1. Mash the mince to separate the pieces and then brown it thoroughly over a high heat. Browning adds flavour. It may be browned in a non-stick pot using its own fat.
2. Once it is browned, add the chopped onions and cook on a lower heat until they are soft.
3. Add the carrots (sliced into circles – they taste best this way as the sweet inner core is intact in each slice) to the mince.
4. Stir in the flour and mix thoroughly.
5. Add enough beef stock or good gravy to cover the mince.
6. Simmer until the mince is tender and the carrots are soft and the gravy is nice and thick – about an hour.
7. Serve with floury potatoes, mashed until smooth with milk and butter.

Following the publication of my work, many letters have poured through the letterbox of my beloved Maison de Mince. It is heartwarming – and yes, you can serve peas with mince.

CHILLI CON CARNE

Just like the "Hot Corn Girls" I told you about (see page 85), not so much later in the 1880s came the "Chilli Queens" with their mariachi street musicians who sold bowls of chilli con carne from street stalls in San Antonio. Texas-style chilli con carne became extremely popular in the south and west of the USA, and is now a favourite across the world. It is just fancy mince, of course.

Ingredients:
>50g butter
>2 large onions, finely chopped
>2 cloves garlic, crushed
>500g lean minced beef
>2 teaspoons chilli powder (half and half with chipotle chilli powder if you have it)
>4 teaspoons ground cumin
>½ teaspoon dried thyme
>½ teaspoon dried oregano
>½ teaspoon ground coriander
>65g tomato purée
>850g tinned red kidney beans, drained (or you can use pinto beans)
>300ml beef stock
>1 tablespoon freshly squeezed lime juice
>Salt and freshly ground black pepper
>Chopped parsley, grated cheddar cheese and chopped red onion, to garnish

Method:
1   Melt the butter in an ovenproof casserole. Add the onions and garlic and fry gently for 5 minutes until the onion turns golden. Stir in the mince and cook, stirring, for 10 minutes.
2   Mix together the chilli powder, cumin, thyme, oregano, coriander and tomato purée and stir into the beef. Add the kidney beans, stock, lime juice and salt and pepper to taste.
3   Cover and simmer for 25 minutes.

4   Sprinkle with chopped red onion, chopped parsley and grated cheddar cheese and serve hot, with plain boiled rice or tortilla chips.

If you can't find chipotle powder, look out for a chipotle pepper sauce and try a dash of this to give a smoky flavour to the dish.

For a veggie version, replace the meat with tofu and add potatoes to the stew.

Serve wearing a poncho, but ask guests to remove sombreros, unless you have a lot of space between the dining table chairs.

A MAIN MEAL WITH PORK

We have respect for pigs. They are intelligent animals. People have the image that pigs are dirty, but they actually keep themselves cleaner than many pets. They lie in mud a lot to cool off as they don't have sweat glands.

PORK CHOPS IN SOURED CREAM

Ingredients:
>   4 pork chops
>   2 tablespoons plain flour
>   30g butter
>   150ml soured cream
>   1 tablespoon lemon juice
>   ½ teaspoon grated lemon rind
>   1 teaspoon sugar
>   Salt and pepper
>   ½ level teaspoon thyme

Method:
1   Dredge the chops lightly with flour.
2   Heat the butter in a frying pan and brown the chops on both sides.
3   While the chops are frying, in a bowl mix the soured cream with all the other ingredients, and add 150ml of water.
4   When the chops have been browned on both sides, take them out of the frying pan and put them into a casserole. Pour the soured cream mixture over the chops.
5   Cover the casserole with a lid or some foil and cook in a moderate oven, 180°C, gas mark 4, for 45–50 minutes.

Parsnips, cut up and roasted in the oven, are a good accompaniment, along with boiled or mashed potatoes.

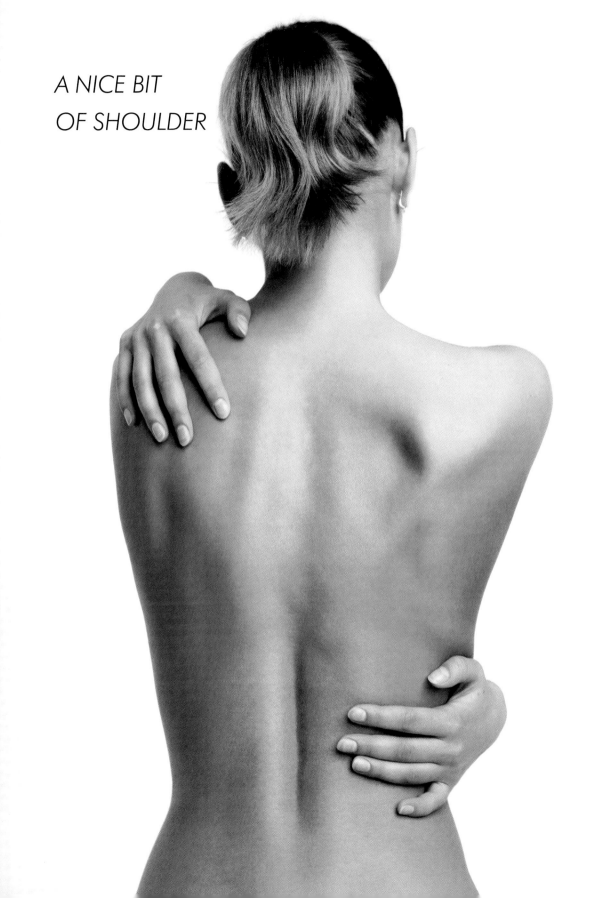

A NICE BIT
OF SHOULDER

STUFFED LOIN OF LAMB

Lamb is a food you can feel good about eating because lamb today is low in fat and a good source of vitamins and minerals and it is easy to prepare, cook and carve.

Mary had a little lamb,
With fleece as white as snow.
And everywhere that Mary went,
The lamb was sure to go.
Mary found the price of meat too high,
Which really didn't please her.
Tonight she is having loin of lamb,
The rest is in the freezer.

You will need:
900g (approximately) loin of lamb (Ask your butcher to bone the meat)

For the stuffing:
120g sausagemeat
90g fresh breadcrumbs
A pinch of dried sage
2 teaspoons finely chopped parsley
1 egg, beaten

For the gravy:
3 tablespoons plain flour
300ml stock (use the water in which you have boiled vegetables)
Salt and pepper

Method:
1   Rinse the joint and pat dry with kitchen paper.
2   For the stuffing, mix the sausagemeat with the breadcrumbs and herbs, and stir in the beaten egg to bind the mixture together.
3   Spread the stuffing over the meat, roll it up and tie it with thin string.
4   Put the meat into a roasting tin and cook in a fairly hot oven, 190°C, gas mark 5, for about 1 hour. Weigh the meat after it has been stuffed, allow 25 minutes to each 450g and an extra 25 minutes.
5   When the meat is cooked through, take it out of the oven, put it onto

a warmed dish and remove the string. Pour off most of the fat left in the roasting tin, leaving about 1 tablespoon. Put the roasting tin on the hob over a medium heat, add the flour, and keep stirring the flour into the fat until it browns.

6   Pour in the vegetable stock and stir until it comes to the boil. Add salt and pepper, and taste to see that you have added enough. The gravy should be fairly thick.

7   Pour the gravy into a warmed gravy boat and serve with the meat.

For lamb, mint sauce or redcurrant jelly are the right accompaniments, served with potatoes and a green vegetable.

FRIED LIVER IN CREAM SAUCE

I have explained about offal (page 19). The easiest offal experience is Fried Liver. Choose one large or perhaps two medium slices of liver per person. Calves' liver is the most expensive, but I think it is the best. Ox liver is the cheapest. Pigs' and lambs' liver cost a little more.

Ingredients:
>   2 pieces of liver per person
>   Flour, seasoned with salt and pepper
>   1 tablespoon oil, such as sunflower oil
>   2–3 tablespoons single cream

Method:
1   Wash the liver in cold running water and dry on kitchen paper.
2   Coat the liver all over with the seasoned flour. This is best done by putting the flour on a flat plate, holding the liver between your fingertips and laying the liver down on one side, then the other.
3   Heat a tablespoon of oil in a frying pan, test that it is hot enough by dropping a little flour ball or crumb in it – it should fry immediately – put in the liver slices, turn down the heat, and fry very gently for 3 minutes each side.
4   When cooked, put it into a warmed serving dish and keep warm.
5   Pour the cream into the remaining oil in the frying pan, which should still be hot but away from direct heat, and stir to make a smooth pouring sauce. Check that it is hot – if necessary stir it over a very gentle heat for a minute, and pour the sauce over the liver to serve.

ROAST BEEF

Ingredients:

A joint of sirloin, rib, pope's eye or silverside
Vegetable oil

Method:

1   Wipe the joint with a clean damp cloth or rinse and pat dry with kitchen paper. Tie it up with string if necessary. Weigh it and then calculate the cooking time. For sirloin, rib or pope's eye, 1 hour 15 minutes for the first kilogram, plus 40 minutes for each extra kilogram. For silverside, 2 hours for the first kilogram, plus 1 hour for each extra kilogram. If you have a piece of beef which is more than 2kg, allow 45 minutes per kilogram, plus 45 minutes.
2   Heat the oil in a roasting tin, sprinkle in a little salt, place the meat in the tin, and baste the cut sides well.
3   Cook in the middle of a hot oven, 220°C, gas mark 7, for 15–20 minutes. Then reduce the heat to 180°C, gas mark 4, and continue cooking until the meat is ready.
4   If you are roasting potatoes with this dish, put them in the oven one hour before the meat is ready, and baste them from time to time.

GRAVY

1   Pour the fat from the roasting tin into a bowl, leaving the sediment in the tin. Separate any meat drippings from the fat and return them to tin.
2   Add 250ml cold water to the roasting tin and skim off any fat which solidifies. Stir well to dissolve all the sediment. Place the roasting tin over the heat on the hob and boil up the gravy. Season and serve in a warmed gravy boat.
3   If you prefer thickened gravy, allow 2 level teaspoons of flour for each 250ml liquid. In a small bowl or cup, blend the flour with a little of the liquid, then stir it into the gravy and bring to the boil, stirring.

STEAK

How do you like it? Cremated, Well Done, Medium, Rare, A Good Vet Could Bring That Back To Life? Cooking time is important. You can grill, or you can pan-fry. The best advice on whether to grill or fry is related to the thickness of the steak.

If you are grilling or barbecuing, the inside of a steak that is less than an inch thick will be dry and tough by the time the surface looks appealingly brown and ready. So – a steak less than an inch thick (2.5cm) should be pan-fried.

The outside of a steak more than 3 inches thick (7.5cm) will be overdone before the centre of the meat is properly cooked. So – piece of meat this thick should be treated like a roast and cooked as one – either as an oven roast or a pot roast. Grilling the perfect steak is an art. It will take practice and considerable patience to become a master. Choose steaks between 1 and 2 inches thick (2.5cm and 5cm) for grilling.

Method:

1   Let your steak relax at room temperature before you grill it, to help it cook more evenly.
2   Trim excess fat off the steak. Half an inch is OK to leave, but cut through the fat strip every inch or so along its length, because, during the grilling process the fat shrinks faster than the meat which causes your steak to curl up, and therefore it won't cook evenly.
3   Brush it with olive oil. Don't pre-season your steak – wait until the final turn. (Ground pepper takes on a bitter taste when scorched, salt can toughen the meat and burnt garlic is horrible.)
4   Preheat the grill.
5   Oil the grid. The best way to do this is to take a piece of trimmed-off fat, hold it in tongs and rub it along the spars of the grid.
6   Place each steak on the grill for one minute. Turn and grill on the second side for an additional minute. Turn and grill for half the remaining cooking time (see below). Turn again.
7   Let the steaks rest for 2 or 3 minutes to allow the juices to settle evenly.

GRILLING TIMES BY THICKNESS

These are total cooking times, so divide in two for each side, and try and ensure that you are fair to each side.

Times are a guideline and will vary depending on the grill, or, if you are barbecuing, on the fuel you are using.

		Thickness		
	1 inch / 2.5cm	1½ inches / 3.75–4cm	2 inches / 5cm
Rare	8 mins (high)	10 mins (high)	12 mins (medium)
Medium	12 mins (high)	16 mins (high)	18 mins (medium)
Well done	16 mins (high)	22 mins (high)	25 mins (medium)

PAN-FRIED FILLET OR RUMP STEAKS

WITH PEPPER / MUSHROOM SAUCE

Cooking time (2cm thick steak):
Rare: 2½ minutes on each side
Medium: 4 minutes on each side
Well done: 6 minutes on each side

Ingredients:
2 lean beef sirloin or rump steaks
1 tablespoon oil

TO MAKE A MUSHROOM SAUCE

50g mushrooms, sliced
2 tablespoons brandy
2 teaspoons Dijon or English mustard
2 tablespoons crème fraîche

TO MAKE A PEPPER SAUCE

1 teaspoon peppercorns, crushed (between two spoons)
2 tablespoons brandy
2 tablespoons low-fat soft cheese
3 tablespoons milk

Method:
1   Heat the oil in a frying pan. Cook the steaks gently, turning to give equal cooking time on each side. Once cooked, remove the steaks from the pan and keep them warm. While you are preparing the sauce, the steaks can breathe and the juices inside will flow from the centre, evenly, within the steak.
2   For the mushroom sauce, add the sliced mushrooms to the pan during the last 2 minutes of cooking the steaks. Add the brandy, mustard and crème fraîche.
3   Heat gently for a few minutes, pour on the steaks and serve.

4   For the pepper sauce, add the crushed peppercorns, brandy, low-fat soft cream cheese and milk. Heat gently for a few minutes, pour on and serve.

These sauces combine very well to make a pepper and mushroom sauce. Serves 2.

SIRLOIN STEAK, PAN-FRIED

WITH BALSAMIC VINEGAR

Ingredients:
> 2 small pieces of butter, 10g each
> 2 tablespoons virgin olive oil
> ½ teaspoon salt
> 1 teaspoon ground black pepper
> 2 sirloin steaks, 1.5–2cm thick
> 1 tablespoon balsamic vinegar

Method:
1   Use a flat skillet or frying pan over a medium heat, and put in the olive oil, one piece of butter, the salt and the black pepper. Heat them together until the butter has melted and the pan is hot.
2   Put the steaks into the frying pan, with fatty edges in the middle of the pan.
3   Cook for 2 minutes on one side, then turn them over and cook for a further minute and a half on the other side (for medium-rare). Allow extra cooking time for medium or well-done steaks.
4   Remove the steaks from the pan and put them on warmed plates to rest for 4 or 5 minutes.
5   Add half a cup of boiling water to the pan and add the second piece of butter and the balsamic vinegar. Stir over a low heat, to reduce the water slightly.
6   Pour the sauce over the steaks and serve. Serves 2.

BEEF WELLINGTON

Ingredients:
>   1.5kg fillet of beef
>   1 tablespoon vegetable oil
>   40g butter
>   225g button mushrooms, sliced
>   175g smooth liver pâté
>   375g puff pastry (see page 181 or buy ready-made)
>   1 egg, beaten

Method:
1   Preheat the oven to 220°C, gas mark 7.
2   Trim and tie up the beef at intervals with fine string, so that it retains its shape.
3   Heat the oil and 15g of the butter in a large frying pan, add the beef and fry until it is sealed and lightly coloured on all sides.
4   Put the beef into a roasting tin and roast it in the preheated oven for 20 minutes. Remove it and allow the beef to cool, then remove the string.
5   Fry the sliced mushrooms in the remaining butter until soft, then allow them to cool and mix with the pâté.
6   On a lightly floured surface, roll out the pastry into a large rectangle to a thickness of 0.5cm.
7   Spread the pâté and mushroom mixture along the centre of the pastry. Place the meat on top in the centre.
8   Brush the edges of the pastry with the beaten egg.
9   Fold the pastry edges over to make a parcel, and turn it over so that the join is underneath, folding the ends under the meat.
10   Place the pastry parcel on a baking tray. Decorate it with leaves cut from the pastry trimmings, and brush with the remaining egg.
11   Bake it for 50–60 minutes, covering it with foil after 25 minutes to stop it getting too brown.
12   Allow the beef Wellington to rest for 10 minutes before serving. Serves 8.

BURGERS

As the Prince of Mince, I can declare with some authority that burgers can be made with just about any sort of minced meat, adding herbs and spices that take your fancy. To bulk up your mince and make it go further, you can add breadcrumbs – but not more than a quarter of the meat content.

To make 6 burgers:

> 250g lean minced meat
> 50g onion, finely chopped
> 2 tablespoons natural yoghurt (I like Greek yoghurt)
> Salt and black pepper
> Olive oil for cooking

Method:

1 Mix together the meat, onion, yoghurt, salt and pepper, then divide the mixture into six parts, making each into a ball. Press it down into a flat burger shape.
2 Before grilling, brush the top of each with oil, place that side down on the grill and oil the top side with some too.
3 Grill for 5–6 minutes each side, turning once.
4 To shallow fry, heat a layer of oil in a pan and fry for the same length of time.
5 Serve in a burger bun or a roll – great with salad and mayonnaise and French fries.

GOURMET BEEF BURGERS

Ingredients:

    1 large egg
    2 tablespoons water
    50ml dry wholemeal breadcrumbs
    1 medium onion, grated
    2 teaspoons English or Dijon mustard
    ½ teaspoon salt
    ½ teaspoon Worcester sauce
    ¼ teaspoon black pepper
    500g extra-lean minced beef (Aberdeen Angus preferred)
    4 hamburger buns, or if you don't have buns use home-made bread and make a sandwich
    Toppings such as cheese, tomatoes, lettuce and dressing

Method:

1. Beat the egg and water together in a bowl, then stir in the breadcrumbs, onion, mustard, salt, Worcester sauce and black pepper. Mix in the minced beef.
2. Shape into four 1cm-thick burgers.
3. Grill your burgers under a medium heat, turning them once, for about 4 minutes each side or until no longer pink inside. (It is OK to break the burger nearly in half on the grill with a fish slice to check how it is doing.)
4. Put the burgers in hamburger buns. Layer with cheese, sliced beef tomatoes, lettuce and salad dressing.

The sandwich is named after the Fourth Earl of Sandwich (1718–92), who was something of a gambler. Sandwiches were made for him so that he could stay at the gaming table without having to get up and go off for meals.

TOAD IN THE HOLE

My Great Uncle Walter used to substitute SPAM (Spiced Ham or Something Posing As Meat) for the sausages during the war. He used to make SPAM fritters as well – slices battered and deep fried. He too was a culinary genius.

Ingredients:

> 15g fat, such as lard or oil
> 240g sausages
> 300ml batter (see page 50)

Method:

1   Preheat the oven to 220°C, gas mark 7.
2   Heat the fat in a baking tin, put in the sausages and bake for 10 minutes near the top of the hot oven.
3   Take the baking tin out of the oven. Give the batter a final beat if it has been standing, and pour it over the sausages.
4   Return the tin to the oven, this time in the centre and with the heat turned down to 190°C, gas mark 5, and continue to cook for 25–30 minutes.

For a complete dinner you could have carrots and a green vegetable, such as Brussels sprouts, with the Toad in the Hole. The batter can take the place of potatoes.

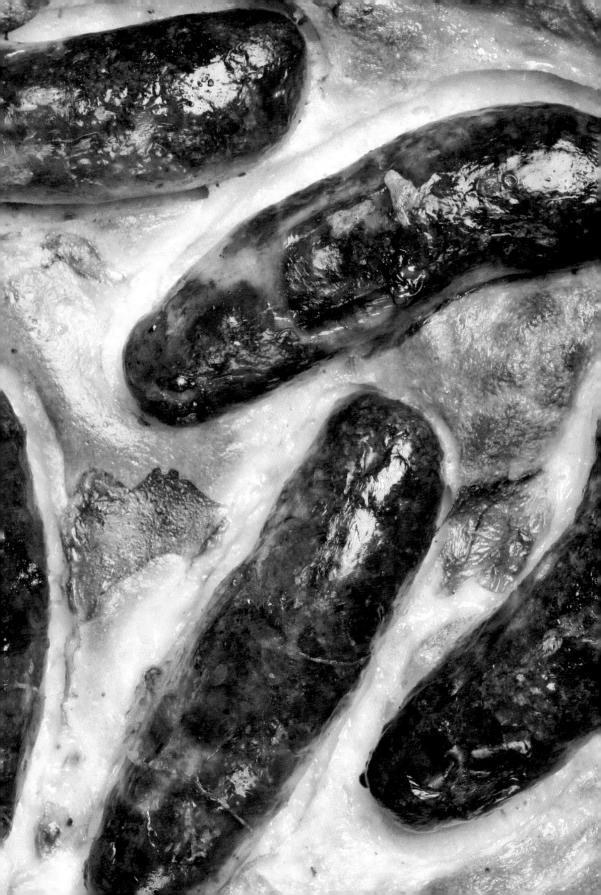

BOUDIN NOIR

If you want to try to make and stuff your own sausages, you may need to invest in some equipment. Just to try it, you can use a large piping bag to get the mixture into the sausage casing. You can buy a machine to do this more efficiently. Some mincers even have a sausage attachment. I know I certainly do. The increase in popularity of sausage-making means that supplies of casings and equipment are quite easy to find should you want to get really enthusiastic.

Boudin is the French term for the famous blood sausage, made with the blood of a pig.

Ingredients:

Open-tubed pork sausage casing 34–36mm diameter, 1.5m long
90g pig fat (lard)
4 medium onions, finely minced
1 large apple, peeled, cored and finely chopped
100g pork fatback (virtually all fat), finely minced
150g lean pork, finely minced
3 cloves garlic, crushed
10g parsley, finely chopped
2½ teaspoons salt
1 teaspoon ground black pepper
¼ teaspoon ground nutmeg
¼ teaspoon ground cloves
¼ teaspoon ground ginger or cinnamon
6 tablespoons full-fat milk
3 tablespoons Calvados (apple brandy)
330ml fresh pork blood

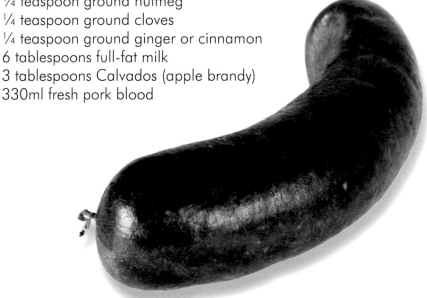

Method:

1 Place the sausage casing in a bowl of warm water for 15 minutes or so, then rinse through the casing with cold running water.

2 In a saucepan with a lid, gently sweat the onions with most of the lard until they become very soft. Drain off the fat and put the onions aside to cool. (Sweating helps onions release their flavours at the beginning of cooking. Use a covered saucepan to do this.)

3 Wipe the saucepan clean, then sweat the apple in the remaining lard for 6–7 minutes. Put aside to cool.

4 Mix together the minced fatback and pork.

5 In a large bowl combine the onions and apple with the garlic, parsley, salt, pepper, spices, milk and Calvados. Mix them all together thoroughly.

6 Add the blood, a little at a time, and mix again.

7 You can now stuff the sausage casing. Once you are ready, put the meat into whatever you are using. Tie one end of the skin and force the meat into the skin. Start with short lengths of skin – not more than 1 metre. Don't overfill, and take care to avoid air gaps. Once you have a long sausage, tie or twist it into individual lengths.

8 Place the sausage length in a pot of cold water and cover with a lid. Bring the water up to near boiling. The boiling point of water is 100°C at standard pressure. You are aiming to poach the sausage for 20 minutes at 90°C. Watch the surface of the water until it begins to boil then turn it down so that the surface is hardly moving.

9 After 20 minutes, take the sausage out of the water and place it on a baking sheet or greaseproof paper. Cool it in the fridge.

Fry boudin noir in a little butter for about 20 minutes together with onion rings and apple slices until they are golden brown. Serve with mashed potatoes.

ROAST CHICKEN

Chickens come plucked, drawn and trussed ready for the oven. Sometimes a whole bird from a butcher will come with a little bag placed inside the chicken containing the giblets (the heart, liver and stomach).

There are a number of recipes that use giblets. If a bird is to be stuffed, the giblets are traditionally chopped and added to the stuffing.

Many breeds of chicken are selected for producing eggs and some are bred for meat alone – others are good at producing both meat and eggs. Chickens farmed for food are tender when eaten. Hens that have lived a long life, crossing many roads, will be tougher, and are better slow cooked.

1 Preheat your oven. See next step.
2 Weigh the chicken and calculate your cooking time as follows. The fast method is to roast it quickly in a fairly hot oven, 200°C, gas mark 6, for 15 minutes per 450g of weight plus 30 minutes extra. The slow method is to roast it at 130°C, gas mark 1, for 25 minutes per 450g plus 1 hour extra.
3 Place the chicken on two slivers of fat (or on lumps of chicken fat) in the roasting dish. Rub all over the outside with salt and pepper. Butter the chicken all over, and put 15g of butter inside the chicken.
4 Roast in the oven. The slow way gives a juicy, tender chicken, which usually has to be finished off for the last 10 minutes at a higher temperature (200°C, gas mark 6) to give a crispy skin. Baste it occasionally during roasting.

ROAST DUCK WITH STUFFING, GRAVY AND ORANGE SAUCE

As we scrubbed the kitchen listening to *Test Match Special* one afternoon, Serge remarked: "I don't understand why anyone wouldn't want to go out for a duck. I always order it."

I started to explain but then ducked out, saying that the English language is full of strange things but he wasn't put off.

"And duck tape? Is it to bind the leg of a lame duck?"

My comment: "No, that's duct tape," was water off a duck's back.

You will need:
>1 whole duck
>Thickened gravy
>Sage and onion stuffing
>Orange sauce

For the stuffing:
>2 large onions, chopped
>50g breadcrumbs
>1 level teaspoon dried sage
>Salt and pepper
>Milk or egg (to bind)

Method:
1. Preheat the oven to 220°C, gas mark 7.
2. Now make the sage and onion stuffing. Bring a pan of water to the boil, add the chopped onions, bring it back to the boil and boil them for 2 minutes, then drain. In a bowl, mix the onions with the breadcrumbs, sage, salt and pepper. Stir in just enough milk or beaten egg to bind the mixture together.
3. Stuff the body cavity of the duck with the sage and onion stuffing.
4. To truss the duck, turn the "apron" under the tail and fix it with a skewer. Truss through the points of wings and through the legs. The finished bird should have a sausage-like shape with none of the joints showing.

5 Prick the skin all over with a fork and rub with salt. Put the bird in a roasting tin, breast side down, and roast in the preheated oven for 30 minutes.

6 Remove the tin from the oven, turn the bird over, and roast for a further 1 to 1½ hours, until it is cooked through.

7 Take the duck out of the oven. Pour off all the fat and make the gravy from the juices.

THICKENED GRAVY

Ingredients:

Sediment and juices from roasting pan
2 level teaspoons cornflour
250ml stock (use chicken stock or vegetable stock from when you boil the accompanying vegetables)

Method:

1 Pour the fat from the roasting tin, leaving the sediment.

2 Put a little of the stock in a cup or small bowl, and blend in the cornflour.

3 Put the roasting tin on the hob over a medium heat. Add the stock and bring to the boil, stirring to scrape up the sediment.

4 Stir the blended cornflour into the stock in the roasting tin, stirring constantly until it boils and thickens.

ORANGE SAUCE

Ingredients:

2 level teaspoons arrowroot or 3 level teaspoons cornflour (arrowroot makes a clearer sauce)
150ml water
Juice of 1 orange
A little sugar

Method:

1 In a bowl or jug, mix the arrowroot or cornflour with a little of the measured water. Boil the remainder of the water and pour it over the blended arrowroot.

2 Add the orange juice, and sugar to taste. Return the mixture to the pan and boil it for 1 minute, stirring until it thickens.

LAMB KEBABS

The kebab is a local delicacy here. I have in the past told you of the King Kebab (life threatening amounts of cadaverous doner kebab meat encased within a supernaturally huge nan bread sarcophagus ... with salad ... delicious).

This is different. We like great big skewers. We like big chunks of meat – not stuff that's been spinning on a rotisserie thingy for a week then shaved off with some sheep shears. We also like lighting fires in our back gardens and charring bits of animals. GRRRRR!

Or use the grill.

Ingredients:
>450g loin of lamb, cut into 2.5cm cubes
>100g mushrooms, halved
>2 rashers bacon, rind removed, cut into 2.5cm squares
>2 onions, sliced into rings
>2 tomatoes, quartered
>4 tablespoons olive oil
>250g rice
>Salt and pepper

>You will need 4 large steel skewers or swords if that is all that's handy.

Method:
1   Spear the first five ingredients alternately onto two skewers, beginning with a piece of bacon, an onion ring, a cube of lamb, a halved mushroom, piece of tomato, another piece of bacon, and so on, until all the pieces are speared on the skewers.
2   Put a pan of water on to boil containing for the rice. Rinse the rice under running water and leave to drain.
3   Turn on the grill to hot. Brush the grill pan with olive oil, sprinkle salt and pepper onto the

kebabs, and dip them in oil poured out onto a flat plate.
4   When the water is boiling, put in a teaspoon of salt, add the rice, reduce heat and cook for 11 or 12 minutes, stirring occasionally to make sure that the rice doesn't stick.
5   When the grill is hot, put the kebabs under it to cook.
6   Turn the kebabs after about 5 minutes, then again after another 5 minutes to make sure they cook evenly on all sides.
7   Drain the rice, and arrange on a warmed serving dish or four plates.
8   Lay the kebabs on top, and pour over the residue of meat juice and oil from the grill pan to serve.

LAMB AND TOMATO CASSEROLE

Ingredients:

> 900g middle neck or best end neck of lamb, cut into cubes
> 240g beef sausages, each sausage cut into 3 or 4 pieces
> 8 rashers streaky bacon, cut into 2.5cm squares
> 1 tin tomatoes (400g)
> 2 sticks of celery, chopped
> 2 onions, sliced
> 1 bay leaf
> Salt and pepper

Method:
1   Put a layer of the meats into a casserole, add a little salt and pepper and cover with a layer of the vegetables. Continue in layers, finishing with some pieces of bacon.
2   Add the tomatoes and, if necessary, a little water so the liquid comes about three-quarters up the contents of the casserole.
3   Cover with a lid and cook in a cool oven, 150°C, gas mark 2, for about 2 hours or until the lamb is tender.

Try cooking thinly sliced potatoes on top of the meat, or serve with boiled potatoes.

My chicken won first prize in a grouse fancy dress competition

GAME

Game is a general term used for wild animals which are used as meat, and includes small animals such as hares and rabbits, birds such as partridge, grouse and pheasant, and large animals such as deer and wild boar. In the war zone, anything is fair game, and gamekeepers keep their heads down. A shotgun does not really challenge le FAMAS – a 5.56 calibre short-range assault rifle fired from the hip – but there are rules in peacetime, and poaching is an offence.

In the 16th century, killing deer meant a death sentence, unless you were in the King's hunting party. In the 18th century and into the 19th, poachers were hanged or sent as convicts to Australia.

Safer to get your game from larger supermarkets, already dressed and ready for cooking. Specialist butchers and farmers' markets are also worth a visit.

You will get the best help from your butcher – ask him to gut it and pluck or skin it for you.

Methods of cooking obviously depend on the type and age of the game.

Older birds, for example, may be tough and should be cooked slowly. Hares and rabbits are best stewed or braised. Venison and wild boar should be cooked in the same way as you would prepare beef or pork.

Here is a selection of recipes that can be adapted.

ROAST PHEASANT

I'm not a pheasant plucker, I'm a pheasant plucker's son.
I'm only plucking pheasants 'till the pheasant plucker comes.

Ingredients:
   1 pheasant
   25g butter
   A few slices streaky bacon (for barding)
   50g fat or oil
   A little flour (for dredging)
   250ml water

Method:
1   Preheat the oven to 180°C, gas mark 4.
2   Pluck (against the grain and after the bird has been hung for two days) and draw (basically, drawing the bird's guts out of its body via its bum and neck openings) the pheasant, if this hasn't been done for you (I recommend getting it done for you. The feathers get everywhere … and the guts thing …). Put a piece of butter inside the body to keep it moist. Truss the bird.
3   Put slices of streaky bacon on the breast, and cover with thickly greased paper.
4   Heat the fat or oil in a roasting tin. Place the pheasant in the tin and cook in the preheated oven for 45–60 minutes, according to the age of the bird.
5   10 minutes before the cooking time is up, take the bird out of the oven. Turn the oven up to 220°C, gas mark 7. Remove the paper from the bird, and baste it with the hot pan juices. Dredge it with flour and baste it again.
6   Return the pheasant to the oven, and roast it for about 10 minutes more, until brown. Take the bird out and place it on a warmed serving dish.
7   Pour the fat from tin, leaving the sediment. Add 250ml cold water, and skim off any solidified fat. Put the roasting tin on the hob over a high heat, bring it to the boil, stirring well, and season.
8   This will give 3–4 servings. Serve it with clear gravy, watercress, game chips or potato crisps and salad.

ROAST PARTRIDGE

We were working one evening listening to Christmas carols.

Serge interrupts the moment: "A partridge in a pear tree? That's ridiculous. Everyone knows that partridges are ground-nesting seed-eaters. I suppose it's just another mistake of hearing. It is supposed to be perdrix – French for partridge."

"A partridge, une perdrix."

"Good King Wences last looked out ..."

"While shepherds washed their flocks by night ..."

"A wean in a manger ..."

Method:
1   Pluck, draw and truss as for pheasant (i.e. get someone to do it for you), putting a knob of butter inside the body to keep the bird moist.
2   Cook as roast pheasant and serve on fried bread with the accompaniments of your choice. Serves 1–2.

ROAST VENISON

Venison is the king of meats and was a favourite of Samuel Pepys who invented the diary.

"I met with Simons and Luellin, and went with them to Mr. Mount's chamber at the Cock Pit, where we had some rare pot venison, and ale to abundance till almost twelve at night, and after a song round we went home."

Sounds like a Saturday night at the Maison de Mince!

Ingredients:
> Haunch, loin or shoulder of venison
> Marinade
> Pork fat (for barding)
> Dripping or butter

For the marinade:
> Olive oil
> Vinegar
> Bay leaf
> 1 onion, sliced
> 1 tablespoon black peppercorns

Method:
1   Marinate the joint for a day in 2 parts oil to 1 part vinegar, with the bay leaf, sliced onion and black peppercorns.
2   When you are ready to cook the joint, remove it from the marinade and drain it.
3   Preheat the oven to 200°C, gas mark 6.
4   Bard the joint with pork fat.
5   Melt the dripping or butter in a roasting tin, put the joint in and put it into the preheated oven. Allow a total cooking time of 30 minutes per 500g plus 30 minutes. After 20 minutes, lower the oven temperature to 190°C, gas mark 5, and continue cooking, basting from time to time. The tin may also be covered loosely with foil, which should be removed for the last 30 minutes of cooking to allow the meat to brown.
6   Serve the venison accompanied by clear gravy, and redcurrant or rowan jelly.

VENISON STEW

Ingredients:
> 500g venison (shoulder, neck or slices from the
> haunch, boned)
> 2 tablespoons plain flour, seasoned with salt and
> pepper
> 25g dripping or butter
> 1 onion, sliced
> 500ml water
> 1 tablespoon redcurrant or rowan jelly

Method:
1   Beat the meat, cut it into neat pieces and coat in well-seasoned flour.
2   In a large stewing pot, fry the sliced onion in dripping or butter, then brown the pieces of venison.
3   Add the water, bring to the boil and simmer very gently for 2 hours or until tender.
4   Add the redcurrant or rowan jelly to the gravy and boil it up. Serve with extra jelly separately.

RABBIT

TO SKIN, CLEAN AND JOINT A RABBIT

Rabbits can be bought fresh or frozen and are usually sold cleaned and skinned ready for cooking. Your butcher can joint it for you.

If you need to skin your rabbit:
1   Cut off the paws.
2   Pull the skin away from the flaps.
3   Push the hind legs upwards through the skin.
4   Cut the skin at the tail and pull the skin up to the forelegs.
5   Push the forelegs through the skin and continue to pull the skin up to the ears.
6   Cut through the ears close to the head and pull the skin off over the head, or the head may be discarded.

To clean your rabbit:
1   Cut off the head, split it open and remove the eyes. Soak the head in cold water.
2   Remove the kidneys, break through the thin skin and pull out the heart and liver.
3   Remove the gall bladder from the liver and discard it.
4   Wash the liver, heart and kidneys.

To joint your rabbit:
1   Divide it into joints as follows:
    2 hind legs
    2 forelegs
    3 pieces of back.
2   Open the ribs up the front and chop into 2 pieces.
3   Wash all thoroughly.

RABBIT SALAD

BROWN STEW OR CASSEROLE OF RABBIT

We argue about the best rabbit stew. Serge says it is Hasenpfeffer – German rabbit stew. The Germans know their game. The French know their onions.

Ingredients:
> 1 rabbit (jointed, with liver and kidneys reserved)
> 1 onion, thinly sliced
> 50g butter
> 3 tablespoons plain flour, seasoned with salt and pepper
> 500ml water or stock
> 1 small apple, chopped (optional)
> 2 cloves
> Salt and pepper
> 50g bacon, fried
> 50g forcemeat, shaped into balls and fried

Method:
1 Joint the rabbit and dip the pieces in seasoned flour. Keep the remaining flour.
2 In a large saucepan, fry the onion in butter until golden brown. Take the onion slices out of the pan and set them aside.
3 Put the joints of rabbit into the hot pan and brown them all over.
4 Add the water or stock, fried onions, reserved liver and kidneys, apple, cloves, seasoning and remaining flour. Cover the pan and simmer over a gentle heat or bake in a moderate oven, 180°C, gas mark 4, for about an hour and a half for a young rabbit, or about two and a half hours for an older rabbit.
5 Arrange the joints on a warmed serving dish, and pour the gravy over. Serve 4–6 with fried bacon and fried forcemeat balls.

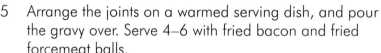

HUMBLE (GAME) PIE

Ingredients for the pastry:
> 200g plain flour
> 100–125g butter
> 1 egg, beaten
> A pinch of salt

Method:
1 Mix the salt with the flour and rub in the butter (see page 31).
2 Make to a stiff paste with the egg, adding a little water if necessary.

Ingredients for the filling:
> 2 pigeons or 1 pheasant
> 6 mushrooms, sliced
> 1 egg, hard-boiled and sliced
> 100g cooked ham or tongue, cut into strips
> Salt and pepper
> 2 tablespoons water
> Some beaten egg, to brush the pastry

You will need a 10cm loose-bottomed pie tin or cake tin.

Method:
1 Preheat the oven to 220°C, gas mark 7.
2 Cut the meat into small pieces, removing bones and skin. Mix the mushrooms, egg, and ham or tongue together, and season.
3 Roll out half the pastry and cut rounds to fit the top and bottom of the tin.
4 Roll out the remainder to fit round the side of the tin.
5 Line the sides, allowing 1cm to lie on the bottom of the tin. Wet the edge and drop in the base. Press down firmly.
6 Place the filling loosely in the prepared mould, piling it high in the centre.
7 Wet round the edges of the pastry sides and cover with the remainder of the pastry. Trim the lid and make a hole in the centre. Brush with egg and decorate with leaves cut out of leftover pastry.
8 Bake on the centre shelf of the preheated oven for 20 minutes, then

reduce the heat to 180°C, gas mark 4, and continue cooking, for 2 hours total cooking time.

To serve hot – fill with stock made from game bones.

To serve cold – dissolve 1 level teaspoon of gelatine in 125ml of game stock, and when almost cold fill up the pie.

Serves 6.

SQUIRREL

SALAD

SQUIRREL STEW

If you would like to cook grey squirrel, ask your local master butcher. Wild meat, low fat, it has a taste, somewhere between lamb, duck and wild boar – a sweet taste because of a diet of berries and nuts. It is illegal to kill a grey squirrel with a bow and arrow or a bomb.

Ingredients:
> 1 grey squirrel, chopped into quarters
> Salt and pepper
> Cayenne pepper
> Olive oil
> 2 dessertspoons vegetable oil
> 1 large onion, diced
> 2 large tomatoes, chopped (or 1 tin tomatoes)
> Assorted fresh vegetables, such as carrots,
> potatoes and parsnips, chopped

Method:
1   Sprinkle salt, pepper and cayenne pepper onto the meat and rub in with a little olive oil.
2   Put 2 dessertspoons of vegetable oil into a large pot and fry the meat together with the onions until well browned.
3   Drain off the excess oil, add about 500ml of water, and bring to the boil. Add the chopped tomatoes.
4   Turn down the heat, and cook gently for an hour. Older squirrels may require cooking longer than an hour. Check by tasting for tenderness.
5   After the meat is tender, add the vegetables. Cook until the vegetables are tender (around 20 minutes).

ANYONE FOR SEAGULL?

Wild birds, including pigeons and seagulls, are protected by law, so you must not harm or injure them. So they can dive-bomb you and there is nothing you can do about it.

Given the abundance of seagulls, I did wonder if there was any way of cooking them – but apparently, what ever you do to seagull it still tastes like rotten fish, and given what these scavenging creatures eat, the very thought of it is quite disgusting.

ROAST A WHOLE PIG

For me the ultimate barbecue experience is to roast a whole pig. I have experience from the front line. We humans have been barbecuing ever since our caveman days when we first rubbed sticks together. Nothing quite like a bison leg or a mammoth steak after a hard day's clubbing, or a tasty young sabre-toothed tiger, stuffed with wild berries, nuts and wild grains, before settling down to a spot of cave painting.

We are fascinated by fire – there is a bit of pyromaniac in all of us. Men can excel at outdoor cooking – a full-body apron, grabbing-tongs in one hand and a fish slice in the other, and we are all set. This is hard work, but is one of the most satisfying tasks I know.

Catching the pig can be a hard and slippery business. Every pig is different, and in the Legion, every fire pit which we dug was different – with different shelter and weather conditions and a variety of fuels, firewood, hardwood, coal or charcoal, all of which can change the length of time the whole performance takes.

You need some bricks to make the walls of the fire pit placed on a suitable piece of ground. You should make a floor for the fire pit – a sheet of metal, maybe a discarded corrugated iron roof. Then fill it with firewood or charcoal and burn it to create embers – you don't want the direct heat of flames because this will burn the skin of the pig too fast. Embers give off radiant heat and you need to spread them evenly across the middle with more at the back end and the shoulder, because the meat is thicker there and takes longer to cook. You will need enough heat to cook the pig slowly for several hours. If your rotisserie is high enough you can have flames, but don't allow the flames to get too near.

You need to make a rotisserie, which can be a metal pole, and you need a means of turning the pole – a hole drilled in one end is best, with a bar through it.

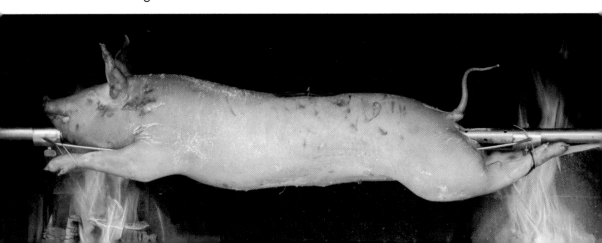

Putting the pig in a marinade can be awkward. My wife was none too pleased to find a dead pig in the bath last time with floating apples and a variety of exotic fruits, so what we do now is use huge heavy-duty plastic bags. She seems to like them better.

The beast needs to be trussed, otherwise it will fall off the pole. As it cooks it loosens. Use wire looped through the back of the pig – the idea is to secure the spine to the pole, tie the head and rear end securely, and use the wire to close the body cavity after the beast has been stuffed with whatever you fancy – whole oranges and lemons, onions, oatmeal – use your imagination.

If you have chicken wire, or fencing mesh, this is great – you can wrap the whole pig in this and, if need be, a twist of the wire here and there during cooking keeps everything nice and tight.

What we are looking to achieve is a beautiful colour and that wonderful caramel glaze on a crispy skin, but not a burnt skin. Apart from keeping flames from the skin, the key is basting to stop the meat drying out.

Olive oil, wine, honey, fruit juices, citrus and vinegar can all be combined with herbs, spices, sugar and salt, but beware of using too much black pepper. Use a paint brush to baste with. (You can use some of the marinade if you managed to get that done.)

VEGETARIAN OPTION

The world record for a giant marrow is about 51kg recorded at the National Amateur Gardening Show.

Each September, the Llanharry Giant Vegetable Championship in Wales attracts some barbecue-sized specimens – and not just marrows! 280kg pumpkins, 33kg swedes and 36kg cabbages!

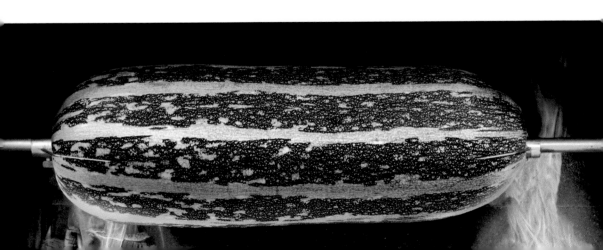

red chillies

paprika

nutmeg

ground ginger

madras powder

turmeric

ground coriander

amchoor (mango powder)

cinnamon

ground cardamom

smoked paprika

black pepper

SPICE IT UP

I learned on the front line that you can curry anything. Curry is the great friend of the Catering Corps when the exact source of the meat is perhaps questionable.

A good curry sauce, served on a bed of carefully boiled rice, decorated with some variety of green leaf (coriander, parsley or bay rather than oak) can hide a multitude of sins, tins and fins, especially when a chunk or slice of a surprise fruit is introduced.

Marinating is about soaking food in a seasoned, sometimes acidic, liquid or yoghurt before it is cooked. It is a bit like pickling – adding flavours by immersing foods in vinegar, for example. Marinating is great for tenderising tough cuts of meat.

You can experiment with lemon juice, wine and different sauces such as soy, and oils, herbs and spices. It is an important part of making a good curry.

Chicken is the most popular choice for "non-veg" Indian friends because poultry gets around the problems of folk who don't eat red meat.

hot chilli powder

annatto (a colouring made from seeds)

white pepper

curry powder

SERIOUSLY HOT CHICKEN CURRY

Before preparing this curry, I suggest you put on some of these disposable gloves, like the ones you get at the local filling station beside the diesel pump, and swimming goggles.

Ingredients:
>3 dessertspoons olive oil
>12 cloves garlic
>2 large onions, chopped
>12 hot red chillies, finely chopped (with seeds)
>1 tablespoon ground coriander
>1 teaspoon ground cumin
>1 teaspoon ground turmeric
>1 cinnamon stick
>500g chicken pieces (breast is best)
>3 tablespoons tomato purée
>250ml chicken stock
>1 dessertspoon balsamic vinegar
>Salt and pepper
>1 teaspoon chilli powder

Method:
1 Start by heating the olive oil in a heavy saucepan and fry the garlic, onions and chopped chillies, coriander, cumin, turmeric and the cinnamon stick, stirring gently with a wooden spoon.
2 Watch the onions – when the onions turn golden stir in the chicken pieces.
3 Fry, turning the chicken pieces with the spoon, and moving them around so that they cook evenly for 4–5 minutes, then add the tomato purée, chicken stock and balsamic vinegar. Stir gently then leave to simmer for an hour, removing and discarding your gloves
4 Towards the end of the cooking time, taste and add salt, pepper and chilli powder. Remove the cinnamon stick.
5 Serve with plain boiled rice (cooked with 10 cloves added at the beginning) and naan bread or roti.

It is the size, not the colour, of a chilli that indicates its spiciness – the smaller the pepper, the hotter it is. The hottest pepper in the world is the Habanero.

At no time touch your eyes (or any other sensitive body parts) with the gloves which have been in contact with the chillies.

CHICKEN CURRY

Ingredients:

    3 cloves garlic, finely chopped
    A piece of root ginger, about the size of a small
    fat cigar, peeled and thinly sliced
    1 teaspoon turmeric
    2 teaspoons ground cumin
    1 teaspoon chilli powder
    1 teaspoon ground black pepper
    8 or 10 cardamom pods
    A handful of fresh coriander leaves (and stalks are
    OK), finely chopped
    500g natural yoghurt
    1 tablespoon honey
    2 tablespoons lemon juice
    A pinch of salt
    1kg chicken breasts, skinned
    4 tablespoons olive oil
    2 medium onions, chopped
    1 small cinnamon stick

Method:

1   In a large bowl, mix the garlic, ginger slices, turmeric, cumin, chilli powder, pepper, cardamom pods and coriander leaves with the yoghurt, honey and lemon juice, adding a pinch of salt.

2   Add the chicken pieces, making sure that the marinade has covered or coated all the chicken, and put it in the fridge for about 6 hours if you can (less is OK – but ensure at least 2 hours to allow the marinade to work its magic).

3   Heat the oil in a large pan, add the chopped onions and the cinnamon stick and fry gently until the onions start to turn a golden colour. Add the chicken and all of the marinade and stir for a minute while bringing the mixture to a gentle simmer. Partially cover with a lid, and simmer for about 30 minutes, tasting and stirring occasionally.

4   Serve with boiled rice – it will take 11 or 12 minutes to boil (toss in a few cloves at the start to give an interesting flavour to the rice). Serves 6.

FRUITY YOGHURT CHUTNEY

A delicious and cooling dip or side garnish suitable for any spicy curry.

Ingredients:
> 250g natural yoghurt
> 1 tablespoon lemon juice
> Tin of guavas or peaches or apricots, drained and
> chopped to small pieces (discard the seeds if you
> are using guavas)
> 1 tablespoon olive oil
> 2 teaspoons mustard seeds
> 1 green chilli, seeds removed, and finely chopped

Method:
1. Mix the yoghurt and lemon juice together and then add the chopped fruit and stir.
2. Heat the oil in a small pan. Add the mustard seeds and cook until the seeds begin to pop. (Make sure you have a lid handy in case they start popping all over the place.)
3. Add the chilli, remove from the heat and stir while the chilli cooks for about half a minute.
4. Pour the chilli, seeds and remaining oil from the pan into the yoghurt and fruit mixture. Cover and chill the chutney.

LAMB CURRY

Ingredients:
> 1kg lamb (boneless)
> 1 tablespoon lemon juice
> 1 tablespoon honey
> 275g natural yoghurt
> 3 tablespoons olive oil
> 2 medium onions, sliced
> 5 garlic cloves, finely chopped
> A piece of root ginger, about the size
> of a small fat cigar, peeled and thinly sliced

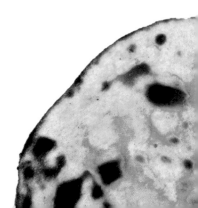

1 small cinnamon stick
10 cloves
10 cardamom pods
2 teaspoons ground coriander
2 teaspoons ground cumin
2 teaspoons chilli powder
1 teaspoon turmeric
A pinch of salt
½ teaspoon freshly ground
black pepper
280ml boiling water
100g blanched almonds
50g shelled pistachio nuts
150ml single cream

Method:

1   Cut the lamb into small cubes. In a large bowl mix together the lemon juice, honey and yoghurt and stir in the lamb. Cover and put in the fridge for 2 hours or more if you have time.

2   Heat the oil and fry the onions, garlic, ginger and the cinnamon stick for 5 minutes, then add the cloves and cardamom pods and fry for a further 2 minutes.

3   Add the ground coriander, ground cumin, chilli powder, turmeric, salt and black pepper and cook for a further minute or so – it will look quite dry.

4   Add the marinade and lamb mixture with the boiling water and stir well. Cover and simmer gently for an hour.

5   Add the nuts and cream and continue to simmer gently for a further 5 minutes.

6   Remove the cinnamon stick. Serve with boiled rice or naan or roti bread. Serves 6.

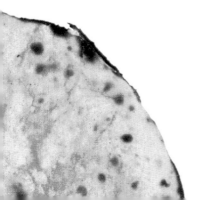

CHINESE STYLE

IMPRESS WITH CHOPSTICKS

It is essential these days to be able to handle chopsticks. It is a sign of a well-travelled gourmet, and necessary if you are not going to starve or miss out at an oriental dinner. If dining out, remember that sometimes the wooden chopsticks come in a little packet, joined together at the end. This is the only occasion when it is acceptable to break the cutlery. Pull them apart to separate them. Don't show your ignorance by trying to eat with them still joined. The diagram shows how to hold and manipulate chopsticks. Serge thinks it is appropriate in Cantonese restaurants to pick up and examine the bill with chopsticks. Even worse, to operate the buttons of the credit card machine with the thin end. Don't do this. Lemon Chicken residue makes the buttons sticky.

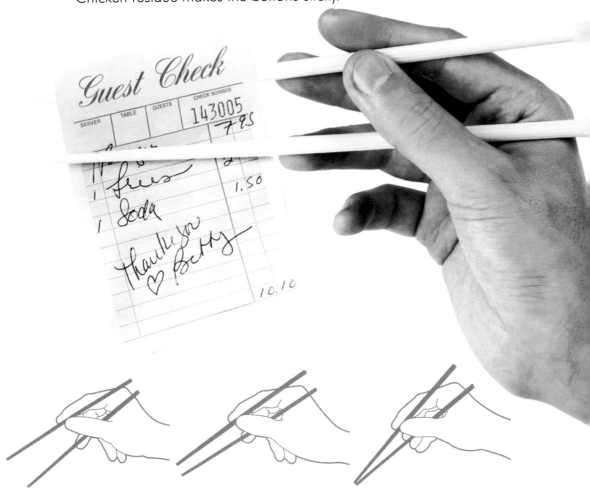

STIR-FRIED PORK, GREEN BEANS AND BEANSPROUTS

Stir-frying is an Asian method of cooking meat and vegetables very quickly, so that they retain good texture and flavour. Stir-frying involves a quick fry over high heat, stirring all the time to cook evenly.

Ingredients:

 1 tablespoon peanut oil (or olive oil with a teaspoon of peanut butter)
 500g pork fillets, thinly sliced
 1 red chilli, finely chopped
 1 tablespoon fresh root ginger, grated
 2 cloves garlic, crushed
 1 teaspoon sesame oil
 2 tablespoons hoi sin sauce (Chinese black bean sauce)
 1 small leek, chopped
 250g green beans, sliced
 2 teaspoons fish sauce
 1 teaspoon cornflour
 1 teaspoon chicken stock powder
 A handful of beansprouts
 150ml water

A wok is an essential piece of kitchen kit these days. At a push you can use a deep frying pan, but get a wok!

Method:
1 Heat half the oil in the wok and add the pork, chilli, ginger, garlic, sesame oil and hoi sin sauce and stir-fry until the pork is tender. Remove the pork and put it aside on a warm plate.
2 Heat the remaining peanut oil and stir-fry the chopped leek and beans.
3 Return the pork to the wok. Add the fish sauce and the cornflour blended with a little water, the stock powder and the water. Stir in the beansprouts, bringing the sauce to the boil to make it thicken a little.

BOILED RICE

To go with most savoury dishes, curries, sweet and sour, or stir-fries, use long-grain rice such as basmati. As a guide, cook 50g of rice (dry weight) per person.

There are many "easy-cook" packs available – generally you put the rice in boiling water and simmer for around 12 minutes. Read the packet!

This is a good method:

Use a liquid measure to measure out the rice, then add twice as much cold water.

If you don't have a liquid measure to hand, a cupful of rice will do two people and add two cups of water.

Put the rice in a pan with the water and add a teaspoon of salt. Stir briefly to separate the rice, bring the water to a boil, reduce the heat to low, put a lid on the pan and cook for 20 minutes (or less for easy-cook rice), until all the water has been absorbed. Take it off the heat and let the pot stand for two or three minutes, then fluff up the grains with a fork and serve.

FRIED RICE

Ingredients:
>5 slices bacon, cut into 1cm pieces (for flavour
>and the oil)
>1 onion, coarsely chopped
>300g cooked white rice
>4 tablespoons light soy sauce
>125g frozen peas
>1 large carrot, finely diced
>A handful of beansprouts
>3 tablespoons peanuts, finely chopped
>2 eggs, lightly beaten
>3 tablespoons spring onion, green tops only,
>chopped
>Cooked chicken, sausage, vegetables or beef
>(optional)

(Note: you can omit the bacon, and instead add 3 tablespoons sesame or vegetable oil for first step, with the onion.)

Method:
1   Partially cook the bacon in a large wok. Add the onion, and fry until tender but not brown.
2   Stir in the cooked rice and soy sauce, and fry until heated through, stirring occasionally. Add the peas, carrots, beansprouts and peanuts.
3   Push the rice to one side. Pour the beaten eggs into the middle of the pan. Stir quickly to scramble the eggs, until they are cooked. Stir the cooked egg into the rice and blend.
4   Add the chopped spring onions and any additional cooked ingredients (chicken, sausage, beef, shrimp or vegetables).

Do not get fried rice mixed up with fired rice which is altogether more dangerous.

PASTA

You need a deep pot full of well-salted boiling water. Add the pasta slowly and carefully, taking care not to break it, and stir to separate it. Cook the pasta until it is tender and slightly firm to the bite – we say "al dente".

But "al dente" or "to the tooth" does not mean that pasta should stick to your teeth! You want it to be firm but not hard. Using salt helps get to the "al dente" texture. It is a balance between it being undercooked (hard in the middle), and overcooked (when it is too soft).

Pasta is made from a paste, which is where the name comes from. Pastes of wheat flour and water and dried pastas were first developed in the Far East and have been around for thousands of years.

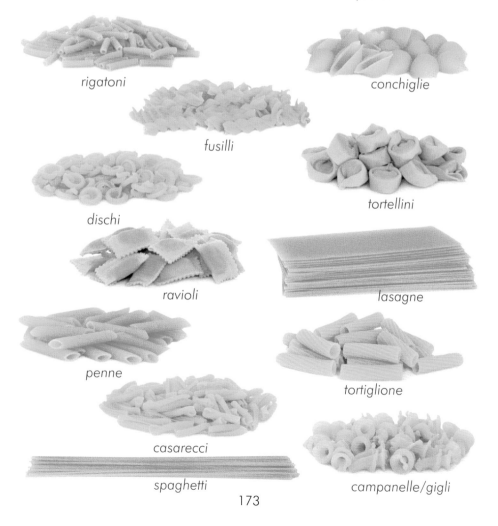

rigatoni

conchiglie

fusilli

tortellini

dischi

ravioli

lasagne

penne

tortiglione

casarecci

spaghetti

campanelle/gigli

TYPES OF PASTA

Why so many kinds of pasta? It's because of the Italian temperament. Italians argue about everything. No-one can agree what shape or what length so they keep on churning out different pastas. Because of temper. That's why the Greeks have so few plates.

* Acomo pepe – small, bead-shaped pasta
* Bucatini – thick, hollow tubes or straws of pasta
* Bumbola – bumblebee-shaped pasta
* Cannelloni – tubes of pasta filled with meat
* Capelli d'angelo – angel hair pasta – thin long-shaped pasta
* Capellini – thin, round strands of pasta
* Conchiglie – pasta shaped like seashells
* Cavatappi – tube or corkscrew or spiral-shaped pasta
* Cresti di gallo – brown pasta, with a curved shape
* Ditali / ditalini – short pasta tubes, like macaroni
* Farfalle – bow-tie shaped medium-size pasta
* Fettucine – flat, wide strands of pasta
* Fusilli – spiral, corkscrew-shaped pasta
* Gemelli – medium-sized pasta, twisted tubes of spaghetti
* Gnocchi – small dumplings, of flour or semolina
* Gomiti – semicircular, short, curved, tubes of pasta
* Lasagne – strips of flat pasta, wavy-edged strips
* Linguine – flat narrow pasta
* Lumache – pasta shells
* Lumaconi – large pasta shells, used with fillings
* Mostaccioli – tubular-shaped pasta
* Macaroni – long or short pasta tubes
* Orecchiette – small, shell-shaped pasta
* Orzo – pasta often used in soups
* Penne rigate – diagonally cut tubular-shaped pasta
* Perciatelli – chunky, hollow pasta strands
* Radiatore – short, chunky, shaped pasta
* Ricciolini – twisted strips of pasta
* Rotelle – spiral-shaped pasta
* Ravioli – pasta parcels, filled with meat or spinach
* Rigatoni – large, ribbed tubes of pasta
* Rotini – spiral-shaped pasta
* Spaghetti – classic round, thin strands of pasta
* Tagliatelle – thin strips of ribbon-like pasta
* Tortellini – neat little pasta parcels with meat filling

* Trenette – long, narrow strips of pasta
* Vermicelli – round, very thin pasta strands
* Ziti rigati – curved medium-size tubes of pasta

SPAGHETTI BOLOGNESE

Ingredients:

25g butter or 1 dessertspoon oil
1 onion, chopped
1 carrot, finely chopped
100g mushrooms, sliced
330g minced beef
40g bacon, chopped
1 tablespoon tomato purée
1 tin tomatoes (400g)
1 clove garlic, crushed
250ml stock
Salt and pepper
A pinch of mixed herbs
200g spaghetti
40g Parmesan cheese, grated

Method:

1. Melt the butter or heat the oil and fry the onion, carrot and mushrooms gently for 4–5 minutes.
2. Add the mince and chopped bacon and brown thoroughly.
3. Add the tomato purée, tomatoes, garlic, stock, salt and pepper, and herbs. Simmer for 30 minutes to 1 hour, stirring occasionally.
4. Cook the spaghetti in boiling, salted water for 10–15 minutes and drain.
5. Place the spaghetti on a hot dish and pour the sauce on top. Sprinkle with grated Parmesan cheese.

PARTY LASAGNE

Ingredients to feed 12 to 14:

9 large sheets of lasagne
500g lean minced beef
250g Italian sausage,
skins removed
1 tin tomato purée (250g)
1 tin tomatoes (400g)
2 tablespoons white sugar
1½ teaspoons salt
1 clove garlic, crushed
3 tablespoons dried parsley,
or a handful of chopped fresh parsley
500g cottage cheese
2 eggs, beaten
½ teaspoon ground black pepper
75g Parmesan cheese, grated
500g sliced mozzarella cheese

Method:

1 Bring a large pot of lightly salted water to a boil. Cook the pasta in boiling water for 8–10 minutes, or until al dente, then drain it.

2 Meanwhile, prepare the sauce. In a large pot or casserole, fry the minced beef and sausage over a medium heat until brown. Stir in the tomato purée, tinned tomatoes, sugar, 1 teaspoon salt, garlic, and half the parsley. Reduce the heat and simmer uncovered for 30 minutes.

3 In a bowl, stir together the cottage cheese, eggs, pepper, Parmesan cheese, the remaining parsley, and half a teaspoon of salt.

4 Preheat the oven to 180°C, gas mark 4. In a lasagne baking dish, layer a third each of the lasagne sheets, sliced mozzarella, cottage cheese mixture, and meat sauce. Repeat the layers twice.

5 Bake the lasagne in the preheated oven for 1 hour, or until hot and bubbly. Let it stand for 15 minutes before serving.

MACARONI CHEESE

S'MAC (short for Sarita's Macaroni & Cheese) is a fine dining establishment located in Manhattan's East Village. What they serve is macaroni and cheese and that's that! Maybe I should open a Maison de Mince across the street to offer a bit of variety?

Ingredients:
>250g macaroni
>4 tablespoons butter
>1 onion, chopped
>1 clove garlic, crushed
>1 tin tomatoes (400g)
>A pinch of grated nutmeg
>Salt and ground black pepper
>125ml milk
>150g Cheddar cheese, grated
>40g breadcrumbs

Method:
1 Cook the macaroni according to the packet directions, and drain it. Preheat the oven to 180°C, gas mark 4.
2 In a saucepan, melt 2 tablespoons of the butter over a medium heat. Add the onion and garlic, and fry gently until the onions have a rich golden colour. Mix in the tomatoes and the nutmeg, and the salt and pepper. Stir in the milk and most of the cheese. Let the sauce simmer gently until the cheese is melted, stirring often. Mix in the cooked macaroni.
3 Transfer the macaroni and cheese mixture to an ovenproof dish. Sprinkle with the breadcrumbs and the rest of the cheese. Dice the remaining 2 tablespoons of butter, and spread it evenly over the top.
4 Bake in the preheated oven for about 45 minutes.

HOW TO MAKE PASTRY

There are many dishes made with pastry so it is important to learn how to make it.

There are many different kinds of pastry – some of the names you will know like shortcrust, flaky and puff, but there is also rough puff pastry, and raised pie pastry (which is sometimes called hot water crust), suet pastry and choux pastry (pronounced "shoo"). This is used to make things like cream buns and chocolate eclairs. There are also several variations of

shortcrust pastry like biscuit crust and flan pastry, and by adding grated cheese to the shortcrust pastry you get cheese pastry, which is used to make cheese straws and many savoury dishes.

One day Serge wants to be pastry chef or pâtissier at the Maison de Mince. He will be skilled in the making of pastry, bread, desserts and in charge of the cheese.

He will be a key member of my brigade de cuisine (which sounds much better than "kitchen staff".

I will give him a badge.

One of the great Scottish delicacies, the Scotch pie, is made with hot water crust pastry. When Serge first came to see me here, I took him on a gastronomic tour of the town. We went into a baker's shop, and there was a big stack of pies on a table near the window. They looked so good that Serge reached out his hand and took one off the top. The baker was furious. That was that wedding cake completely ruined.

SHORTCRUST PASTRY

As shortcrust is the most usual we should begin with it, but first remember these points:

1   Sift the flour to be sure it is not lumpy and let the air into it.
2   Rub the fat into the flour with tips of your fingers. Lift the dry mixture well out of the bowl and let it run back through your fingers. This, again, is to get air into the mixture.
3   Use cold water and measure it. Too much will make the dough sticky and difficult to roll and the pastry will be tough. Use a knife to mix it in if you have used the rubbing in method.
4   Do not handle the dough more than you can help, and when you roll it, avoid putting a lot of flour on the board, and roll in short sharp rolls. It is not necessary to grease the baking tin when baking pastry.

CORNISH PASTIES

This is not a pie. It is a wrap of pastry, filled and sealed and made like a parcel, then cooked.

We remember a soldier from Cornwall who joined the Legion and gave his name as Teddy Oggin.

That's what they call a Cornish Pasty in Cornwall. He married a London girl called Ruby Murray, left her, and is greatly missed.

For the shortcrust pastry:

> 250g plain flour
> ½ level teaspoon of salt
> 125g fat (half butter and half lard or vegetable fat)
> 2 tablespoons water

For the filling you need:

> 150g frying steak or good quality stewing steak, diced
> 1 medium potato, diced
> 1 small onion, finely chopped
> Salt and pepper
> 1 tablespoon water
> A little milk or beaten egg

Method:

1. Sieve the flour and salt into a bowl.
2. Rub in the fat with your fingers until the mixture is like fine breadcrumbs.
3. Add the water, and mix with a knife until the mixture clings together.
4. Gather it into a ball with your fingers.
5. Turn it out on to a lightly floured board and knead it lightly until smooth. Cover it and let it stand in a cool place for 30 minutes.
6. Preheat the oven to 220°C, gas mark 7.
7. In a bowl, mix together the diced meat, potato, onion, salt and pepper. Add the water and mix well.
8. Divide the pastry into 4 pieces and roll each into a round about 15cm across, which is the size of a small tea plate. Trim the edges using the plate or a saucer as a guide.
9. Put a quarter of the meat mixture on each round and damp round the edge of the pastry with milk or beaten egg.
10. Fold the pastry over and press the edges well together. Using your thumb and first finger, flute this edge.

11　Put the pasties onto a baking sheet with the fluted edge uppermost. Brush with milk or beaten egg and bake in the preheated oven for 25 minutes, then lower the heat to 180°C, gas mark 4, and bake for another 25 minutes, so that the meat will be well cooked.

12　Serve with mashed potatoes or cold with salad.

PUFF PASTRY

Ingredients:

>　225g plain flour
>　1 teaspoon lemon juice
>　½ teaspoon salt
>　Cold water
>　225g unsalted butter

Method:

1　Sieve the flour and salt together into a bowl.

2　Make a well in the middle of the flour and add the lemon juice. Stir with a knife, adding enough water to make an elastic dough.

3　Place on a floured surface and knead gently for 5 minutes, until the dough is smooth and does not stick to the fingers.

4　Roll out the dough to form a piece large enough to cover the butter, then place the butter (straight from the fridge) in the middle of the dough.

5　Fold over the ends over one at a time.

6　Flatten in one or two places using a rolling pin, then roll out gently and evenly into a long strip, ensuring that the butter does not come through or come from between the edges.

7　Fold one third towards the middle, then the remaining third into the middle to form three layers, pressing down gently. Do not seal the edges.

8　Leave the pastry to rest in a cool place for 15 minutes.

9　Place the pastry on a floured surface, so that the unsealed edge is towards you, roll and fold again as before.

10　Turn and repeat three more times.

11　Leave the pastry to rest in a cool place for 10 minutes.

12　Place the pastry on a floured surface, so that the unsealed edge is towards you, roll and fold again as before.

13　Turn and repeat three more times. The pastry is now ready for use.

DANGEROUS DESSERTS

We use the word desserts rather than puddings, because pudding can mean something else, like Yorkshire pudding or suet pudding, black pudding or steak and kidney pudding, which are disappointing with custard.

ORANGE CREAM

Ingredients:
> 125ml natural yoghurt
> 2 tablespoons orange marmalade
> A squeeze of lemon juice
> 1 tablespoon brown sugar

Method:
1   Mix the ingredients together and chill before serving in a fancy glass with a long spoon.
2   Optional – serve with wafers / sponge fingers.
3   Optional – grate some dark chocolate and mix with the other ingredients, and save some crumbs to sprinkle artistically on the surface.
4   Optional – vodka, mixed in, or on the side, chilled to near frozen.

STUFFED PINEAPPLE

Ingredients:
    1 large pineapple
    2 oranges
    Cherries or strawberries
    2 tablespoons sugar
    1 tablespoon Cointreau (bitter orange liqueur)

Method:
1. With a strong, long knife, slice off the top of the pineapple. Scoop out all of the pineapple flesh, but take care to keep the walls of the pineapple intact.
2. Remove the hard core and cut the pineapple flesh into small pieces.
3. Peel the oranges, separate into segments and slice into small pieces.
4. Place into a bowl with the pineapple, and add the sugar together with the cherries or strawberries and the Cointreau. Leave to soak for an hour or so in the fridge.
5. Before serving, spoon the fruit back into the pineapple shell and replace the pineapple lid.
6. Serve with a small glass of Cointreau.

BAKED APPLE

Ingredients:
> 4 large regular-shaped cooking apples
> 4 teaspoons raisins
> 4 teaspoons jam or marmalade
> A little sugar

Method:
1. Put a little water on to boil in the whistling kettle.
2. Preheat the oven to 200°C, gas mark 6.
3. Core the apples (this means boring a hole from the stalk end right through to the other side, and taking the core out – you can use a potato peeler, turning it as you bore through), and fill each hole with the raisins and jam or marmalade.
4. Place the filled apples in an ovenproof dish. Slit the peel on each apple in two or three places. When the water in the kettle boils, pour some of the water over the slits, then sprinkle the apples with a little sugar. Bake for 30–40 minutes in the preheated oven.
5. Take the apples out well before they are to be eaten as they will be very hot, and serve with cream or ice cream.

TRIFLE

I get infuriated with Serge's child-like questions about the English language. He knows perfectly well what "Don't trifle with me" means.

So I said to him: "A trifle is something of no significance – just a cold dessert made with sponge cake spread with jam or fruit, soaked in wine or sherry, covered with a custard sauce and cream – no different from a custard pie which can be upturned on your head with ease. Like this!"

Ingredients:

1 sponge round or packet of sponge fingers
Raspberry or apricot jam
6 tablespoons sherry or 125ml fruit juice
Sliced fresh fruit, such as bananas, peaches, strawberries
250ml pouring custard (you can buy this in the supermarket)
125ml whipping cream
½ teaspoon vanilla essence
Sugar to sweeten cream

Method:

1 If using a whole sponge, cut it into slices. Spread the slices or sponge fingers liberally with jam and place them in the bottom of a 1 litre dish or bowl. Arrange the sliced fruit on top.

2 Pour the sherry or fruit juice over the sponge and fruit.

3 Pour the custard over the sponge and fruit leave it to soak for at least 30 minutes.

4 Add the vanilla essence to the cream and sweeten it to taste with a little sugar. Whip the cream until it stands in soft peaks.

5 Use a piping bag to pipe the cream on top of the custard, or spoon it on carefully. Decorate the top of the trifle with small sweets, or a few extra strawberries.

BAKED ALASKA

This dessert will delight and impress. It will serve up to 6 people, unless they are greedy, and some will be disappointed. Portion control is required. It does have to be prepared at the last minute before eating.

Baked Alaska is also known as a Norwegian Omelette. February the 1st is Norwegian Omelette Day, which I suppose is a bit like Pancake Tuesday?

Ingredients:

> 1 tub of ice cream (family/large size),
> A large slice of cake (just larger than the ice
> cream block)
> 2 egg whites
> 3 tablespoons caster sugar

Method:

1   Switch on the oven and really blast it to its hottest temperature (mid-day Sahara).
2   Whip the egg whites until they are stiff, then fold in the caster sugar, making a meringue mixture.
3   Lay the cake slice on an ovenproof dish. Spread the ice cream on it, and top with the meringue mixture, taking care to seal in all the ice cream. Put it into the oven to bake for 6–7 minutes. (The top should be just turning golden brown.)
4   Take it out and serve it without delay.

CRÈME BRULÉE

Ingredients:
>500ml double cream
>1 teaspoon vanilla extract
>1 heaped tablespoon caster sugar, plus 6
>tablespoons for topping
>4 eggs yolks

You will need about six ramekins to serve this dessert in. Ramekins are small glazed ceramic or glass serving dishes made to withstand high temperatures, as they are frequently used in ovens, or in this case when the recipe is finished with the use of a cooking torch flame.

Method:
1   Preheat the oven to 150°C, gas mark 2.
2   In a small saucepan, gently bring the cream and vanilla to a simmer.
3   Remove the pan from the heat and let the mixture cool for at least 10 minutes.
4   In a large bowl, beat together the egg yolks and caster sugar until creamy in texture and light yellow in colour.
5   When the cream has cooled, slowly beat it into the egg mixture with a whisk.
6   Divide this custard mixture between the ramekins and place them in a baking dish large enough to hold them all. Pour boiling water into the baking dish so that it comes halfway up the sides of the ramekins.
7   Place the dish carefully in the preheated oven and bake for 30 minutes or until the crème brulée has set lightly.
8   Remove from the oven, allow to cool and chill in the fridge for 2 hours.
9   About 30 minutes before you are ready to serve, spoon a thin layer of caster sugar on top of each ramekin of custard. Use a cooking torch to heat the sugar, which will fuse, creating a hard top on the custard. Alternatively, preheat the grill to hot and put the ramekins under the grill for 1 minute. Watch them constantly during this process, as sugar burns very easily.
10   When the sugar has melted, carmelised and cooled, serve.

TREACLE TART

There's no treacle in treacle tart. You British…

For the pastry:
>   250g plain flour
>   ½ level teaspoon of salt
>   125g fat (half butter and half lard or vegetable fat)
>   2 tablespoons water

For the filling:
>   6 tablespoons golden syrup (or substitute jam or
>   lemon curd)
>   25–30g fresh breadcrumbs
>   1 teaspoon lemon juice

You will need a pie plate about 20cm in diameter.

Method:
1   Sieve the flour and salt into a bowl.
2   Rub in the fat with your fingers until the mixture is like fine breadcrumbs.
3   Add the water, and mix with a palette knife until the mixture clings together.
4   Gather it into a ball with your fingers.
5   Turn it out on to a lightly floured board and knead it lightly until smooth. Cover it and let it stand in a cool place for 30 minutes before rolling it out.
6   Shape the remaining dough into a ball and roll it out into a round a little larger than the plate.
7   Lift it up on the rolling pin and line the plate, pressing the pastry down well. Trim the edges and press all round with the prongs of a fork.
8   Put the syrup, breadcrumbs and lemon juice into a small pan, stir over a low heat and mix well together, then turn it on to the pastry.
9   Roll out the remaining piece of dough into a round, and cut across three times, which will give you six triangles. Arrange these neatly on top of the tart, then bake in the centre of a fairly hot oven, 190°C, gas mark 5, for about 30 minutes. Serves 6.

TIRAMISU

Tiramisu means "pick-me-up" – "a wee stiffener" as they would say round here, but cleverly disguised as a dessert. This is one of those desserts that you can add things to – mainly alcohol – and make your own. If you are Italian all recipes different to your own mother's will be wrong.

Ingredients:
>   200ml espresso coffee
>   A small glass of Amaretto (an Italian sweet
>   almond-flavoured liqueur)
>   1 teaspoon vanilla extract
>   3 tablespoons brandy
>   250g mascarpone cheese
>   4 tablespoons caster sugar
>   1 packet sponge fingers
>   Cocoa powder or 1 large plain chocolate bar,
>   grated

Method:
1   Make the espresso coffee, let it cool and pour it into a large bowl. Stir in the Amaretto.
2   In another bowl, whisk the vanilla, brandy, 50ml of the coffee, mascarpone and caster sugar.
3   Dip half the quantity of sponge fingers in the coffee and Amaretto liquid and lay them on the bottom of a serving dish, covering the dish. As you dip the fingers in the liquid, let them absorb the liquid but not disintegrate.
5   Spread half of the mascarpone mixture on top of the layer of fingers.
6   Prepare a second layer of sponge fingers dipped in the liquid, and place them in the dish.
7   Spread the remaining mascarpone mixture on top and sprinkle with the cocoa powder or the grated chocolate.
8   Put the dish in the fridge and chill for 3 hours before serving.

LEMON POSSET

The Possets are a family of drinks and desserts which includes Eggnog – a milk-based punch called after a small drinking cup called a noggin. Not to be confused with Noggin The Nog who was a kindly king in Viking times.

Ingredients:

 850ml double cream
 125g caster sugar
 2 large lemons, rinds grated and juice squeezed
 Grated rind of 1 large lemon, to serve

Method:

1 Put the cream in a saucepan along with the sugar. Bring it very slowly to the boil and simmer very gently for 3–4 minutes.
2 Take the pan off the heat, then whisk in the lemon juice and the finely grated lemon rind.
3 Pour the mixture into six dessert dishes or glasses and chill them in the fridge for 3 hours.
4 Sprinkle the tops with grated lemon rind before serving accompanied by Scottish shortbread fingers, to applause.

PINEAPPLE SORBET

'Sorbet' in English is a fruit flavoured water ice used in posh dinner parties to 'cleanse the palette' between courses. If you have crowns or sensitive teeth, avoid it and cleanse with more wine.

Ingredients:

 1 large pineapple
 1 tablespoon rosewater
 1 tablespoon sherry
 2 tablespoons maple syrup
 1 egg white
 A pinch of salt
 A few drops vanilla essence
 Mint sprigs, to garnish

Method:

1 Cut the top off the pineapple with a large sharp knife, then halve and quarter it lengthways. Cut the skin off each quarter and cut out the core.

2   In a blender or food processor purée the pineapple, adding the rosewater, sherry and maple syrup.
3   Beat the egg white with a pinch of salt and the vanilla essence until it is nearly stiff, then stir it into in the pineapple purée.
4   Spoon the mixture into a freeze-proof container and put it in the freezer for 3 hours. Take it out and stir it with a fork two or three times during that time.
5   When you are ready to serve the sorbet, spoon it into four wine glasses or dessert glasses. Garnish with a sprig of mint.

FRUIT CRUMBLE

Ingredients:
>   675g cooking apples, such as Bramley
>   4–6 tablespoons sugar
>   A strip of lemon peel or 2 cloves

For the crumble:
>   60g unsalted butter, chilled
>   120g plain flour
>   120g granulated sugar

Method:
1   Preheat the oven to 190°C, gas mark 5.
2   Peel and core the apples, cut into small pieces and cook with the sugar, the lemon peel or cloves, and about 3–4 tablespoons water.
3   When the apples are cooked, remove the lemon peel or cloves and put the fruit into a pie dish.
4   Rub the butter into the flour, add the sugar and sprinkle the mixture on top of the fruit, pressing it down firmly.
5   Put the dish into the preheated oven, just above the centre, and bake for 30 minutes or until the crumble topping is lightly browned.

Variations:
1   Mix sultanas with the apple before putting it in the pie dish.
2   Add a little mixed spice to the flour.
3   Sprinkle some finely chopped nuts on top of the crumble mixture before it goes in the oven.
4   Vary the fruit according to the season. Blackberries go well with the apples in summer.

CHOCOLATE DOORSTEP

The Chocolate Doorstep is in fact a Breton dance. Apart from weddings and celebrations, dancers were called in to stamp on the earth floor of a new dwelling. These dances could go on for hours, fuelled by chocolate pudding and Calvados.

Ingredients:
>1kg tin unsweetened chestnuts
>Oil for greasing
>250g plain chocolate, chopped
>250ml water
>175g unsalted butter, softened
>175g caster sugar plus 1–2 tablespoons for serving
>3 tablespoons brandy
>350ml double cream

Method:
1   Purée the chestnuts in a blender or food mixer with 3 tablespoons of the liquid from the tin.
2   Grease or oil a loaf tin, 7.5x10x20cm. Line the bottom with greaseproof paper and oil the paper.
3   In a small saucepan, melt the chocolate in the water over a low heat and cook, stirring, until it is the consistency of thick cream. Let it cool. Cream together the butter and 175g of caster sugar until soft and light. Stir in the chocolate, chestnut purée and 2 tablespoons of the brandy.
4   Spoon the mixture into the tin and cover it with greaseproof paper. Put it in the fridge for 24 hours.
5   When you are getting ready to serve, tip out the block onto a serving plate or tray, peeling away the paper.
6   Whip the cream until it stands in peaks, then beat in the extra sugar and 1 tablespoon of brandy and whip it again until it is stiff. Using a piping bag, pipe most of the cream around the base and on the top of the block. Serve the remainder of the cream on the side.

GOLDEN SPONGE PUDDING

Ingredients:

120g unsalted butter, softened
120g caster sugar
2 eggs, beaten
120g self-raising flour
3 tablespoons golden syrup

Method:

1   Cream the butter and sugar together until the mixture is soft and light.
2   Add the beaten eggs to the creamed mixture alternately with the sifted flour. Mix lightly together.
3   Put the syrup into the bottom of a buttered 1 litre pudding basin. Spoon in the mixture and cover it with greased paper or foil.
4   Put the pudding basin into a steamer or into a pan half-filled with boiling water and steam for about 25 minutes. Alternatively, why not use 6 175ml minature basins. Cook for about 20 minutes in a roasting pan filled with water in the oven 180°C, gas mark 4.
5   To serve, turn out onto a hot dish and top with a little more hot syrup and a walnut to garnish.

Variations:

1   Use jam instead of syrup.
2   Add 1 teaspoon ground ginger to the flour.
3   Substitute 1 tablespoon cocoa for the same amount of flour and omit the syrup.

COFFEE CUPCAKES WITH CHOCOLATE TOPPING

For the cakes:
>   175g self-raising flour
>   175g caster sugar
>   175g unsalted butter, softened
>   3 large eggs
>   45ml espresso coffee
>   75g pecan nuts, chopped

For the syrup:
>   30ml hot espresso coffee
>   50g light muscovado sugar
>   A dash of Amaretto liqueur

For the topping:
>   100g mascarpone cheese
>   50g milk chocolate, melted and cooled

Method:
1   Find your Meccano set. The Advanced set is best.
2   Select the pieces as per the diagram and create your Cake Stand. If your Cake Stand is motorised (recommended) and you are using remote control, ensure that you have the correct weight balance to ensure best performance.
3   Preheat the oven to 180°C, gas mark 4.
4   In a large bowl, whisk together the flour, sugar, butter and eggs, until smooth and fluffy.
5   Fold the coffee and chopped nuts into the mixture.
6   Divide the mixture between 12 paper cake cases set in a cake baking tray. Put in the preheated oven and bake for 15 minutes or until risen.
7   While the cakes are baking, put the finishing touches to the Cake Stand, then stir the sugar, hot espresso and Amaretto together in a jug to make a syrup.
8   As soon as the cakes come out of the oven, pierce them in several places with a skewer and drizzle over the syrup.
9   Leave to them cool on a wire rack, then whisk the topping smoothly together and decorate – perhaps with more nuts (the edible kind).
10   Take care with liquids to avoid rust developing on the Cake Stand.

DEATH BY CHOCOLATE CAKE

Ingredients:

> 225g dark semi-sweet chocolate (40–50 per cent cocoa)
> 140g unsalted butter
> 4 eggs
> 210g caster sugar
> 4 heaped tablespoons plain flour
> 4 tablespoons unsweetened cocoa powder
> 1½ teaspoons baking powder
> 1 teaspoon vanilla essence
> 4 tablespoons soured cream

Method:

1 Preheat the oven to 180°C, gas mark 4.
2 Line a round 25cm (8cm high) cake tin with greaseproof or other non-stick paper and grease the tin. Or you can use two shallow cake tins, lined and greased.
3 Break the chocolate into small pieces and put it in a bowl with the butter. Set a pan of hot water on the hob, and place the bowl over it. Carefully melt the chocolate and butter, making sure the hot water does not boil over.
4 In a large bowl, beat the eggs with the caster sugar, then mix in the flour, cocoa powder, baking powder and vanilla essence.
5 Gradually fold in the melted butter and chocolate mixture, and then the soured cream.
6 Spoon the mixture into the prepared cake tin and put it in the preheated oven. Bake for 40–50 minutes, until a wooden pick or a skewer inserted in centre comes out clean. (If using two shallow cake tins, 20–30 minutes may be sufficient.)
7 Take the cake out of the oven and leave it in the tin. When it has cooled to room temperature, put it in the fridge to chill for at least 30 minutes before removing the cake from the tin (the cake is sticky and difficult to cut when it is warm!). With a sharp knife, remove the crusted surface from the top of the cake, and cut it in half horizontally.

ICING

Ingredients:

160ml double or
whipping cream
260g dark semi-
sweet chocolate
(40–50 per cent
cocoa), finely
chopped

Method:

1   Put the cream into a saucepan and heat it gently.
2   Remove it from the heat, add the finely chopped chocolate, and stir until the chocolate melts and it is smooth. Let it cool until it thickens.
3   Spread a third of the icing between the two layers and sandwich them together. Spread another third on top, and the rest around the sides of the cake. Put the cake into the fridge for 1 hour or more to set the icing.

Serve the cake at room temperature.

CLEVER WITH CHEESE

Cheese is a brilliant option for afters if you are not quite there yet with your Lemon Posset.

You can even get dairy-free cheese for vegan entertaining, for sauces, pizza toppings and salads.

A carefully arranged and selected cheeseboard shows a level of sophistication and you can go two ways: "less is more" – perhaps a little Brie served with a teaspoon of runny honey drizzled onto the plate with some walnuts on the side, or a blue cheese with thin apple slices. The problem with "more than less" is that it is a little over the top and you are obliged to explain what each of the cheeses is – and whether it is from goat's milk or some remote Italian hillside or churned by peasant farmers in Argentina. Avoid notices on cocktail sticks stabbed into each variety.

Extraordinary stuff, cheese. Apart from savouring amazing flavours and textures, you can use it to bait mice, of course, but you can fight malaria with it too. A ex-comrade in the Corps, from Tanzania, tells me that they have been buying Limburger cheese – a cheese that reeks of terribly smelly feet – by the container load.

Apparently the African mosquito goes for your ankles as it loves the smell of human feet, and they use the cheese to lure the little biters away from you. Presumably you have a little trolley thing that you pull behind you with a lump of cheese on it. Alternatively you could wash your feet.

The first choice on my cheeseboard is Emmental – but our Swiss cheese gets some flak. The US Department of Agriculture (USDA) came up with guidelines to regulate the hole size of domestically produced Swiss cheese. They reduced the standard size of the holes because new cheese-slicing machinery was getting caught on the bigger holes. We Swiss were not at all pleased. It is a yellow, medium-hard cheese, with characteristically large holes. It has a piquant, but not very sharp taste. Different types of bacteria are used, and towards the end of the cheese production process, the cleverest bacteria devour the lactic acid produced by the other bacteria, forming carbon dioxide gas which blows into bubbles which make the holes.

In the unlikely event of unwrapping your Emmental and finding it imperfect, simply shoot holes in it from different angles.

MAKING A CHEESE FONDUE

Fondue is the Swiss signature dish, a dish for friends, a sharing experience. A pot is heated over a small burner, and guests use long forks or skewers to plunge pieces of food into the warm semi-liquid cheese mixture.

There are numerous different kinds of fondue, but usually an aromatic blend of wine, different cheeses and seasoning are used.

Prepare the pot by rubbing it with some garlic. Take a large clove and split it and rub it all over the inside. Add the wine and the cheeses and stir gently until the cheese has melted. Add a little flour to stop the liquid separating – you can use cornflour or ordinary flour.

Allow 100ml of white wine per person (dry white is best) and a 200g mix of cheese – try Gruyère hard cheese blended with Emmental or Raclette. Pieces of bread, apple slices and other delights which can be stabbed onto a skewer are then dipped into the mixture.

Napkins are essential.

CHEESEBOARD

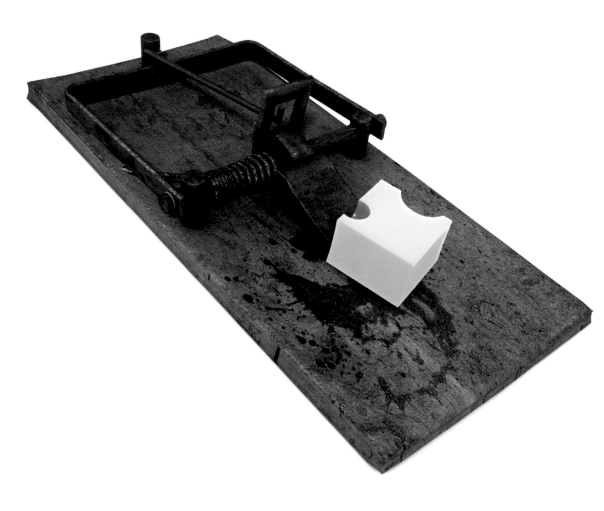

CAVIAR

Some folk would say that caviar is a little old-fashioned – a bit James Bond, perhaps. Caviar is marketed across the world as a delicacy and can be served as a garnish or as a spread, with hors d'oeuvres. Caviar is simply sieved and lightly salted fish roe (eggs).

Sturgeon roe is generally thought to be the "true" caviar.

There are four types of caviar to argue about: beluga, osetra, sterlet and sevruga. The rarest and most expensive is from the beluga sturgeon that is found in the Caspian Sea, but there has been a sharp decline of sturgeon populations there, which have led to conservation measures. Sterlet caviar is rare and once upon a time was exclusively prepared for Russian tsars, Iranian shahs and Austrian emperors. Osetra is of lesser quality, as is sevruga caviar.

Caviar varieties produced from farmed sturgeon and paddlefish in the USA and Europe are environmentally sustainable and are the best option. Many worthy chefs like myself agree that farmed caviars are indeed comparable to the finest Caspian varieties.

Caviar should be served simply, perhaps with lightly toasted bread (soft, not hard like crackers), with lemon wedges, capers, some very finely chopped onion and hard-boiled, chopped egg.

A chilled unflavoured vodka or glass of champagne is an ideal accompaniment.

TRUFFLES

Truffles are fungus – expensive fungus (up to £2,000 per kg expensive). Truffles are sniffed out by female pigs, who can detect the smell that is also in the saliva of male pigs. The same chemical is present in the sweat of the human male.

WHEN THINGS DON'T GO TO PLAN

… and everything was ready. Mussels – to be beautifully cooked in a plunge of white wine, to be drizzled with cream and a confetti of parsley … the Beef Wellington baking proudly in a medium oven, the pastry glaze a masterpiece of heart shapes and pastry leaves … the table setting "just right"! Crisp linen tablecloth – the cigarette burn cleverly masked with the condiments tray, held in position with double-sided duct tape.

The doorbell rings. An impatient ring. She's early – but we're all set! The wine is open. What can go wrong? She sweeps into the room – stunning! Leg-hugging designer jeans, and pointed red PVC shoes that would burst a football on contact. The T-shirt – pastel shades with print front and back – what was that slogan? "Vegan and Proud" … Oh s**t!

BAKED BEANS

Open the tin and pour out the beans into a small saucepan, scraping every last one out of the tin with a wooden spoon. Heat gently for a few minutes, then divide evenly into two portions. Serve immediately. Beans should be eaten with a fork.

Serves 2.

Warning: Baked beans are known on occasion to cause a considerable increase in flatulence following consumption.

APPENDICES

AT THE TABLE

Good table manners are essential. These days even young children are expected to be able to use a knife, fork and spoon properly.

We must eat our food with appropriate cutlery. Learn the formal table setting. You hold the fork in your left hand and the knife in your right hand (or the other way round if you are left-handed). Above your place setting will be a dessert spoon and perhaps a dessert fork.

At a very formal dinner party, perhaps you will have many knives forks and spoons. Use the cutlery on the outside first and work inwards with each subsequent course.

The foods we don't eat with cutlery include finger foods, canapés, sandwiches, crisps, corn on the cob, and of course fruit. Eating pizza and chicken with your fingers is acceptable at a picnic or barbecue, or in a very informal setting.

People in other countries do eat with their hands. We often have visitors to the Maison de Mince from Hyderabad. They like my Lamb Biryani. They eat it with their fingers like they do at home. Very clever – great finger action. Use the right hand (only) and make the biryani into little towers – it is sticky enough to hold together between your fingers, and pop the tower into your mouth.

Even if you are extremely hungry, don't put too much food in your mouth at a time. Chew small quantities and swallow all the food in your mouth before scooping up more or taking some water or wine. It is embarrassing if someone at the table asks you a question and you have a full mouth and it takes a long time to chew and despatch everything, by which time you have forgotten the question. It is even worse to imagine that you can speak with your mouth partly full. And don't chew with your mouth open and don't slurp. It should not need to be stated that you should not try to speak with a mouthful of wine.

Between mouthfuls, conversation is polite, but don't sit there pontificating, holding your fork and knife in the air, gesticulating with them – rest the fork and knife on your plate.

Don't stretch across the table with your knife and dig into the butter and then butter your bread with the same knife. There should be a butter knife. Take some butter from the butter dish and delicately place it on your side plate, then you can butter pieces of your roll a little at a time. This is to stop the butter dish getting full of crumbs.

Never put your knife in your mouth or lick it or use your fingers to load up your spoon or fork.

If you want to put your knife down, and just eat with your fork, you can turn your fork over. You change hands when you do this, so if you are right-handed you eat with the fork in your right hand.

Once you have finished eating, and as a signal – to your host or a waiter – that you have indeed finished, put your knife and fork together on your plate (fork prongs pointing up, and away from you).

Don't attempt to pick food out of your teeth with your fingernails or a business card. If there are toothpicks on the table and you really, really have to get rid of the strands of beef or duck that have lodged between your teeth, use a toothpick, or excuse yourself and head for the restroom or bathroom.

If soup is served, to eat it, select the soup spoon – the one with more of a rounded shape to it – and tip the bowl away from you and spoon the soup up to your mouth. But don't fill the spoon, and remember to eat from the side of the spoon – don't open wide and put the whole thing in your mouth.

Eating peas and some beans and pulses can be a challenge. You can stab them with your fork, prongs down, or look for something with adhesive properties on your plate – some mashed potato, for example.

If all else fails, put down your knife and transfer your fork to your other hand, and adopt a shovelling technique, pushing the peas against some meat or solid vegetable to get them onto your fork.

To eat dessert, take your fork in the left hand, and have your spoon in the right hand. Tackle the dessert with your spoon, one bite at a time. Use your dessert fork to push the food onto your spoon. Eat from the spoon.

DINNER PARTIES

As a dinner party host you should ask in advance if your guests have any special dietary needs – perhaps they are allergic to fish or nuts. Perhaps they have no teeth.

As a guest if you cannot eat a particular kind of food or have some special requirement, inform your host several days before the dinner party. Do not provide your host with recipes or meal suggestions.

On arrival always venture to ask your host or hostess "Is there anything I can do to help in the kitchen … perhaps open the tins?"

It is normal to take a gift of some sort to give to your host when you arrive. Wine is perhaps the most usual, but beware of leaving it to the last minute and avoid the corner shop adjacent to your host's home as it is likely that

VALUE BEANS

NET WT 15.5 OZ (439g)

your host will be aware of the current 3 for 2. Best to find a remote stockist and select a bin-end that no one has ever heard of.

Flowers are an option, but again beware of the local filling station's offering. A modest bunch will not have your host collapsing with hay fever. Best not to take something you have baked, as the host will feel obliged to serve up your gift at some stage.

Pre-dinner drinks can be dangerous. If you are used to having a few gin and tonics served in a hotel or public house, with measures that are almost undetectable beneath the questionable aerated tonic, beware of the generous host who thinks he is being kind and virtually fills the tumbler with gin.

As a guest, when seated at the dinner table and food is served, it is essential to wait until your host lifts his cutlery to begin eating or at least indicates that you can begin.

Your host will most probably have baked bread or rolls and served them attractively in a basket. It is essential that you try these and make appropriately enthusiastic remarks. Break a piece from a roll before buttering it and eating it. Similarly, cut a piece of bread into smaller pieces. Eating it whole is not a good idea.

Always say thank you when served something. Always comment on how wonderful it is.

Any uneaten food should be neatly pushed to the side of the plate. Don't attempt to cover uneaten fish or meat with a lettuce leaf or bury it in mashed potato to pretend you have eaten it. If you have not eaten everything that was put in front of you, then you must make it clear that it wasn't the food that was not good or not well-cooked (even if that was the case). Better to lean back in your chair, pat your belly and say "I'm stuffed" or "that was just too much for me!" If you are from the Legion you might say, to impress, "Je suis hors de combat!" (out of the fight, surrendered), but don't be too smart and get it wrong – a coup de grâce is a death blow intended to end the suffering of a wounded man; and a coup de main is a swift pre-emptive strike.

Having declared yourself hors de combat after the main course, you need to manoeuvre cleverly to suddenly be fit for dessert. Some remark such as "There is always room in the pudding department" will suffice.

THE NAPKIN

We have regular visitors to Maison de Mince. They are called the Slitter Brothers.

Whatever food is put down in front of them, they slitter down their shirts. It is a problem when your belly is so big that you can't see the plate and the journey of the spoon from the soup plate to your mouth takes on the excitement of a roller coaster ride, guided by a shaky hand. Why is it that they are so fat and still need to diet, when only 50 per cent of the food they order ever makes it down their throats?

That's why the older Slitter Brother wears a bow tie – it is out of range.

It is thanks to the Brothers that I have adjusted my thinking on the rules of the use of the napkin. I always thought that tucking a napkin into your clothing was considered "common", and that a napkin should be delicately placed across your lap, but fashionable men of the 18th century wore stiff collars, which required protection best afforded by a napkin or bib tied around their neck. This is where the expression "to make ends meet" comes from. Similarly, to protect collar shirts with button fronts which became fashionable, napkins were tucked in at the neck or were attached with a clip.

I say it is perfectly acceptable to protect one's clothes with a bib or napkin to save on embarrassment at table, and a host rushing for some dab-on stain remover every few minutes. Better to boil-wash a linen napkin than a designer suit or dress.

The absolute rule, however, is that a napkin or bib should never be used to blow your nose with, and it should not be used to wipe your teeth.

WINE

I love cooking with wine. Sometimes I even put it in the food.

Wine is an alcoholic drink which is made from the fermented juice of grapes or from a variety of fruits and plants. Serge, as you know is an expert.

Wine is produced by crushing the grapes and allowing them to ferment with yeast, which absorbs the natural sugars found in the grapes, converting them into alcohol. Grapes have a natural chemical balance, which allows them to ferment without other nutrients such as sugars, enzymes or acids.

There are many different kinds of wine, which are made from different varieties of grapes, and various yeasts are chosen depending on the type of wine in production.

Many other fruits such as apples and berries can also be fermented in this way. The resulting wines take the name of the fruit from which they are made – apple wine, elderberry wine and raspberry wine, for example – and they are generically known as fruit wines. Other wines are made from starch-based ingredients: for example, rice wine and barley wine. They are closer to beers and spirit-based drinks than fermented wines.

The term "wine" refers to the alcohol content, rather than the production process itself.

Dessert wines are sweet wines typically served with dessert, such as Sauternes and Tokaji Aszú. Despite the name, they are often best appreciated alone, or with fruit or bakery sweets.

There is no simple definition of a dessert wine. In the UK, a dessert wine is considered to be any sweet wine drunk with a meal, as opposed to the white fortified wines (fino and amontillado sherry) drunk before the meal, and the red fortified wines (Port and Madeira) drunk after it. Most fortified wines are regarded as distinct from dessert wines, but some of the less strong fortified white wines, such as Pedro Ximénez sherry and Muscat de Beaumes-de-Venise, are regarded as honorary dessert wines.

The very best thing to do is to try different wines and don't think that the biggest prices mean the best wines. Look for recommendations – ask your local wine merchant. I think it is perfectly acceptable to explore within price bands, and make up your own mind.

Me? I look for a good multi-buy!

I like French, of course – but among my favourites are some of the Italian reds, particularly the Sangiovese grape – and if you spot any red from Sicily or Puglia you are unlikely to be disappointed. I was guilty of favouring quantity over quality, but as I get older, I have come to like some of the big Italian wines – Brunello, Barolo and Chaos, for example. If you are ever in Imola, in Italy, ask Leonardo at Osteria Callegherie to tell you about wine. You'll be there all day.

Or ask a Slitter Brother – there are many around. The more stained the tie or shirt the more expert the wearer.

Boudin is the name given to a Legionnaire's blanket roll.
We've discovered it's also an excellent wine warmer.

OVEN TEMPERATURE CHART

A manufacturer always supplies a temperature chart with the cooker, so see if you can find yours and study it carefully. First set the oven to the required number or temperature, then turn on the heat and allow about 15 minutes for the oven to reach the right temperature. As a rule, in a gas cooker the top of the oven is the hottest part and the bottom the coolest, while in an electric oven the bottom is nearly as hot as the top and the centre is the coolest part.

The chart below is a guide to how hot the oven would be at a certain setting:

Gas	Conventional electric	
0–1	110–130°C/225–250°F	very cool or slow
1–2	140–150°C/275–300°F	cool or slow
3–4	170–180°C/325–350°F	warm
4–5	180–190°C/350–375°F	moderate
5–6	190–200°C/375–400°F	fairly hot
7–8	220–230°C/425–450°F	hot
9	240–260°C/475–500°F	very hot

In fan ovens the air is heated at the back and spread evenly throughout the oven so there are no cooler or hotter areas. Therefore, the temperatures needed for cooking in a fan oven are lower than those required in a conventional electric or gas oven (see chart below). You will probably find that as well as adjusting temperature, you will need to deduct cooking time.

Temperature comparison in °C

Conventional oven	Fan oven
130	100
150	120
180	140
200	160
225	180
250	200

USEFUL WEIGHTS AND MEASURES

As ordinary tablespoons vary in size, it is best to use the British Standards Institution spoon. The levels in the list opposite have all been measured with the BSI tablespoon. Your own tablespoon might be a little different, but if you use the same spoon for measuring all the ingredients the proportions will be correct.

To measure a half spoon, fill the spoon level, then using the tip of a knife, divide it down the centre longways. For a quarter spoon, divide the half across.

3 level tablespoons flour	= 30g (1oz)
2¼ level tablespoons caster sugar	= 30g (1oz)
2½ level tablespoons icing sugar	= 30g (1oz)
3 level tablespoons cocoa	= 30g (1oz)
3 level tablespoons cornflour	= 30g (1oz)
2 level tablespoons cheese (finely grated)	= 30g (1oz)
1 level tablespoon jam	= 30g (1oz)
1 level tablespoon golden syrup	= 30g (1oz)
2 level tablespoons rice	= 30g (1oz)
1 breakfast cup flour (loosely packed)	= 120g (4oz)
1 breakfast cup sugar	= 240g (8oz)
1 breakfast cup currants (loosely packed)	= 240g (8oz)
1 breakfast cup fresh breadcrumbs	= 90g (3oz)
1 breakfast cup liquid	= 300ml (½ pint)
8 tablespoons milk or water	= 150ml (¼ pint)

SAFETY IN THE KITCHEN

Accidents can happen very quickly, but most can be prevented.

1   Always make sure that your work surface is clear and clean before you begin preparing food.
2   If you spill anything on the floor, wipe it up at once.
3   If you spill or splash any fat on the cooker, wipe it off immediately.
4   When you leave saucepans on the cooker, check that all the handles are turned towards the back of the cooker. If they are sticking out, someone passing might easily knock them over, or a child might get hold of the handle and scald itself.
5   Use padded oven gloves to remove hot tins and dishes from the oven.
6   Before carrying pans from the cooker to the sink, look to see that no one is in the way and that there is plenty of room to stand the pan down when you get to the sink.
7   Be sure to turn off all gas and all hob switches when you have finished cooking.
8   If you burn yourself or cut your finger, let someone attend to it at once.
9   If you are opening a tin, be very careful that you do not cut yourself on the edges.
10 Always be very careful when you are using a sharp knife and put it away after you have finished using it.

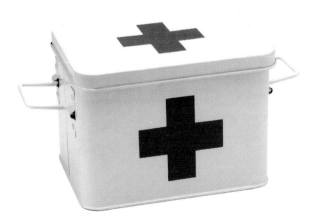

INDEX